POLICY STUDIES IN EMPLOYMENT AND WELFARE NUMBER 29

General Editor: Sar A. Levitan

Jobless Pay and the Economy

Daniel S. Hamermesh

The Johns Hopkins University Press, Baltimore and London

Copyright © 1977 by The Johns Hopkins University Press

Manufactured in the United States of America

The Johns Hopkins University Press, Baltimore, Maryland 21218
The Johns Hopkins Press Ltd., London

Library of Congress Catalog Card Number 76–47369
ISBN 0–8018–1927–X
ISBN 0–8018–1928–8 (pbk.)

Library of Congress Cataloging in Publication data will be found on the last printed page of this book.

Contents

Preface vii

1. Economic Implications and Statutory Provisions 1

2. Who Pays for UI Benefits and Who Receives Them? 10

3. The UI System and the Worker 31

4. The UI System and the Employer 59

5. Other Economic Issues 79

6. What Do We Know and What Should Be Done? 97

Notes 109

Bibliography 112

Tables

1. Unemployment-insurance Provisions as of January 1975, Selected States 3

2. Replacement Measures, Selected States, 1974 18

3. Characteristics of the Unemployed (Survey) and the Insured Unemployed (State Programs), March 1973 and March 1975 22

4. Studies of the Effects of UI Benefits on the Duration of Unemployment 35

5. Estimated Supply Effects of Selected UI Policies on the Unemployment Rate   52

6. Studies of the Countercyclical Effects of UI Benefits and Taxes   63

7. Percentage of Paid Employment Covered by State UI Programs, 1939, 1960, 1973, by Industry   84

8. Estimated Total Effects of Regular State UI Programs on the Civilian Unemployment Rate   100

Preface

This monograph was commissioned by the National Council on Employment Policy. The readers from that group, Professors Sar Levitan and Gerald Somers, provided useful and detailed comments on the study at several stages of its development. However, neither they nor the National Council are in any way responsible for errors that may remain, nor do they necessarily subscribe to the policy changes I have proposed.

After this book went to press the UI Amendments of 1976 were enacted. The major provisions were a rise in the tax base to $6000; an increase in the Federal tax to .7 percent, and an extension of coverage to most state and local employees. Our arguments and recommendations are not greatly altered by the first two legislated changes, but the increase in coverage almost entirely incorporates our recommendation on this issue.

Throughout the execution of this study I was aided by my former colleagues at the U.S. Department of Labor. Particularly helpful were Edward Fu and Joseph Hight of ASPER, and James Vanerden and Steven Wandner of the Unemployment Insurance Service, who supplied comments and unpublished data at several points. Where there is no source listed for a title or for some unpublished data, it should be understood that the Unemployment Insurance Service of the U.S. Department of Labor produced the material.

Ronald Ehrenberg, Robert Goldfarb, Frances Hamermesh, Belle Landau, Richard Lester, Robert Taggart, and Ruth Witty made numerous comments on the style and substance of the work. Perhaps most helpful have been the many individuals who have written on the detailed issues in the unemployment-insurance program. Only those studies that provide specific information relevant to the discussion are referenced in the text; many others were consulted and excluded because of limitations of space. The study's completion was expedited by Matthew and David, who stayed downstairs.

Jobless Pay and the Economy

1

Economic Implications and Statutory Provisions

In September 1974 the White House Conference on Inflation was held. At one session, attended by many of the leading economists in the United States, employment and welfare programs received substantial attention. Only unemployment insurance (UI) was commented on approvingly by all who mentioned it.[1] This contrasts sharply with the negative impressions the public often receives from the media and some economists.[2] Which view is correct or do both opponents and proponents miss the whole truth because they fail to understand the institutions of UI and are ignorant of its effects? Providing the background for an answer to this question is the essential purpose of this book.

We do know that UI is a major government program. Benefit payments grew from one-half billion dollars in 1939 to nearly 17 billion in 1975. They vary greatly over the business cycle, declining as economic conditions improve. Even in a boom year like 1973, though, UI benefits were .46 percent of the income consumers had to spend or save (disposable income). In 1975, the trough of the 1973–75 recession, benefits were over 1.5 percent of disposable income. This figure exceeded 3 percent of all federal, state, and local government spending and constituted over 13 percent of all transfer payments paid by governments to individuals. Although small relative to the gross national product, UI clearly is major among the nation's employment and welfare activities.

Implicit in the disagreement among economists and others are differences over policy issues of current and recurrent interest: eligibility and duration of UI benefits; methods of financing payments and apportioning the tax among those groups that do pay; and variations among states in the amount and duration of benefits. Most fundamental is the question of the appropriate federal role in unemployment insurance. Economic analysis can shed light on all of these issues. Economics—both theoretical and empirical—has much to say about policy in this area. For some of the issues the evidence is clear-cut or the analysis fairly simple. For others the lack of evidence or the complexity of the analysis required makes it impossible to draw any but the simplest or most tentative conclusions.

The converse is also true: The UI system may have substantial effects in those areas in which economists are most interested, such as unemployment and the allocation of resources. For example, UI can affect the behavior of an unemployed individual or an individual currently not in the labor force by making work more attractive to him. The taxes paid by employers to finance UI can also affect employers' willingness to take on new workers or lay off current employees.

Although the UI system was mandated initially by the Social Security Act of 1935, most of the taxes that finance the system are raised by the individual states, and the benefit levels, duration, and rules surrounding the receipt of benefits are also determined by the states. This makes it impossible to try to comprehend the nuances of all the various state programs and still analyze the underlying economic issues produced by the general similarities among the different programs. However, some detailed institutional knowledge is necessary. In this book we present as much detail as is needed to appreciate the economic problems in UI policy without obscuring the discussion with an excess of minutiae.[3]

Table 1. Unemployment-insurance Provisions as of January 1975, Selected States

	Colorado	Massachusetts	New York	Oregon	South Carolina
Minimum base-period employment or wages	30 x weekly benefits; $750	$1200	20 weeks; $600	18 weeks; $700	1-½ high-quarter earnings; $300
Potential duration of benefits (weeks)					
1. Minimum	7	9	26	9	10
2. Maximum	26	30	26	26	26
Tax rates					
1. Minimum	0	.5	.3	.8	.25
2. Maximum	3.6	5.1	5.2	3.2	4.1

SOURCE: *Comparison of State Unemployment Insurance Laws*, January 1975.

Who Receives Unemployment Benefits and How Much Is Paid?

In order to understand the main general features of state UI systems let us consider a person who has just been separated from his firm. (The state could be one of the fifty states, the District of Columbia, or Puerto Rico.) Immediately after separation he (or she) files an *initial claim* for benefits at a local Employment Security office. Upon receipt of this claim the office must determine three things. First, is the former employee covered by the state UI system? Essentially all who are employed in manufacturing firms would be covered, but those working in agriculture, the self-employed, domestic household workers, and persons employed in certain state and local government activities or in certain small nonprofit operations probably would not be covered and thus would be ineligible for benefits. (Railroad workers, ex-servicemen, and federal employees are covered by small, special programs which we will ignore in this discussion, and there are minor interstate differences in coverage.)

Second, is the claimant *eligible* for benefits? Eligibility is defined in terms of prior work attachment and the reason for separation. The regulations on prior work attachment differ from state to state, as table 1 indicates. Among the five states used as examples throughout this book Colorado requires the worker to have earned thirty times the *weekly benefit amount* and $750 in the *base period*. (In thirty-five states in 1975 the base period was the first four of the five calendar quarters preceding the filing of a claim; in most of the remaining states, including Massachusetts and New York, it was the fifty-two weeks preceding the claim or the receipt of benefits.) In Massachusetts a flat amount of annual earned income is required for eligibility; in New York and Oregon there are requirements for both weeks worked and earnings in the base period; and in South Carolina the claimant must have earned 1.5 times his *high-quarter earnings* and $300 during the base period. Other states use different criteria for eligibility, but these examples illustrate the main types of provisions. The purpose of all such provisions is to ensure that the individual has a strong attachment to the labor force and is really interested in finding work.

The other criterion for eligibility in most states is whether or not the worker quit or was laid off for cause. If he quit voluntarily or was fired, he will be declared ineligible, although this decision can be appealed. In a few states such workers will receive UI benefits after a long waiting period (usually six weeks or more).

Third, if the individual is eligible for benefits, the office must determine what his weekly benefit amount is and how long he may receive it (his *potential duration* of benefits). Potential duration is uniform in eight states (including New York), but in others it varies depending on the claimant's base-period earnings and/or weeks of employment. In most states the *maximum potential duration* is twenty-six weeks. Weekly benefits may be some fraction of a worker's high-quarter earnings (Colorado, Massachusetts, and South Carolina), a variable fraction of his average weekly wage during the base period (New York), with the fraction equal to .5 in most cases, or a portion of his entire base-period earnings (Oregon); or some other method of determination may be used. In eleven states, including Massachusetts, the claimant can also receive extra benefits (*dependents' allowances*) linked to his weekly benefits, his base-period earnings, and the number of dependents in his household. In all states there is a *maximum weekly benefit*, which cannot be exceeded regardless of prior earnings or work history. This maximum is defined either in dollar amounts or relative to the state average weekly wage in covered employment (in thirty-two states, including Colorado, Massachusetts, Oregon, and South Carolina). This maximum is not higher than two thirds of the state average weekly wage except in those states where dependents' allowances are also paid.

When the claimant returns (after the one-week *waiting period* in all but eight states), assuming he has not been disqualified, he is told what his weekly benefit is; when he must report to pick up his benefit check, or in some states, when it will be mailed to him; and what his potential duration is. In most cases both potential duration and amount of benefits depend on the individual's attachment to the labor force. Every two weeks (in most states) the beneficiary returns at the appointed time to receive a check for his UI benefits, which are not taxed. If he moves elsewhere, his claim will be filed *interstate*, with the charges assessed against his former location and his check receivable at his new location.

So long as he can show he is looking for work and that he has not refused *suitable work* in a job found for him by the Employment Service, the worker may continue to receive his payment. *Suitable work* is necessarily an ambiguous term, and its interpretation is subject partly to the discretion of local UI officials. In general, it is work that uses the skills employed on a previous job. In all states except Montana the beneficiary may take part-time work and receive partial benefits up to his potential duration. If the beneficiary has not found suitable work by the end of the period equaling his potential duration, he is said to have *exhausted his regular benefits.*

The major changes in the UI system since 1969 have involved the maximum potential duration of benefits. In 1970 the Federal-State Extended Unemployment Compensation Act became law. It provides *Extended Benefits* automatically if the *insured-unemployment rate* in a state (benefit claimants as a percentage of total covered employment) is at or above 4 percent and at or above 120 percent of the average of its level in the same three months in the past two years. (Congress generally has waived the 120-percent restriction through laws enacted on an ad hoc basis.) The program also operates on the state level if it is triggered by national unemployment conditions. As a result of Extended Benefits a worker now can receive benefits at his same weekly rate for an additional period equal to half of his potential duration under the regular state program, or thirteen weeks at most.

In December 1974 and March 1975 additional Federal Supplemental Benefits were enacted providing up to twenty-six more weeks of benefits at the same weekly rate if an individual exhausted his benefits under the Extended Benefit program. (The potential duration is twice that for which the beneficiary was eligible under the Extended Benefit program.) Payments cease entirely if a state's insured-unemployment rate falls below 5 percent. A recipient could conceivably draw UI benefits for sixty-five weeks under the combined regular and extended programs—Extended Benefits and (temporary) Federal Supplemental Benefits. In addition to the latter program, which expires in March 1977, a temporary *Special Unemployment Assistance* program was also enacted. Effective as of July 1975, it provides up to thirty-nine weeks of UI benefits for workers whose base-period employer was not covered. Thus a claimant declared ineligible because his base-period employer was not covered could still receive the same weekly benefits for a limited potential duration under Special Unemployment Assistance if he were not ineligible for other reasons. In 1975 payments under all extended programs totaled $4.6 billion, while $12.0 billion was paid under regular state programs.

Where Do the Funds Come From?

In 1975 the federal unemployment tax was 3.2 percent of wages up to a *tax base* of $4,200 in earnings per annum. The tax is collected by the federal government from employers. In only three states—Alabama, Alaska, and New Jersey—is there also a contribution by the employee. The tax applies to employment in a given firm; if an employee quit a $8,400-a-year job on July 1 and a replacement was hired immediately, the firm would pay a double tax for that year, since it would pay up to the $4,200 ceiling on each of the job's two incumbents. Its *taxable wages* for that job would be $8,400. The tax base was $3,000 from 1939 until 1972, at which time the higher, $4,200 base went into effect. However, states have been free to impose a higher tax base for their own systems, and six states (including Oregon) had a base above $4,200 in 1975.

The greater interstate variation is in the determination of the *tax rate* paid by the firm. The federal law allows states to void most (currently all but .5 percentage points) of the 3.2-percent federal tax. The states are then free to construct sets of schedules that vary the tax rate charged to individual plants so long as overall financial solvency is maintained. (These schedules are said to be *experience rated*, and only one schedule is in effect in any one year.) If a state's benefit payments have been a small fraction of taxable wages in covered employment *and* the state varies tax rates across plants, it is free to have an average tax rate below the 2.7 percent (3.2 minus .5) that the federal law allows as a reduction in payments by employers. (The .5-percent federal tax is used for various purposes, to be discussed below.)

Almost all states use some type of experience rating of employers to fix the rate paid on the taxable earnings of their employees. The tax rate varies depending on the employer's past experience and the overall solvency of the entire state system. If a firm has a high layoff rate and a large fraction of its former employees receive UI benefits after separation from the plant, its tax rate will be higher. As can be seen from table 1, the possible degree of variation differs substantially among states. Indeed, in 1975 the most favorable schedule in Colorado allowed firms with a good unemployment experience to pay no taxes, while on the least favorable tax schedule the maximum rate was 3.6 percent. Colorado is one of the thirteen states in which the minimum rate on the lowest schedule was zero in 1975. Maximum rates on the highest tax schedule varied from 2.7 percent in some states to as high as 8.5 percent in others.

Determination of the tax rate depends upon the type of system used. Under one method, used by thirty-two states in 1975, taxes are paid into each firm's account, and benefits are distributed from it. The ratio of the cumulative balance to annual taxable wages in the plant is called the *reserve ratio*. When it reaches a certain level (usually determined in relation to highest annual benefits paid out over a period of ten years or longer), the firm receives a reduced tax rate. If the firm is being taxed at the minimum rate, further charges on its reserves cannot lower its rate unless the entire tax schedule is lowered. Similarly, if its balance is so low as to place it at the highest rate, extra charges will not affect its rate unless the entire tax schedule is raised.

If the employer has a negative balance in his reserve account, the typical recipient's benefits are paid from a general state pooled fund. In effect, payment is then shared by all firms in the state. Similarly, if the benefits are *noncharged*—for example, because the individual quit his job but received payments after the waiting period—the funds come from the general pool. If the entire state is in negative balance, its officials can arrange a loan from federal unemployment-insurance trust funds (financed by the .5-percent federal tax or by loans to the funds from general revenues) to use in paying out benefits that are due. If there is time, however, a state will first shift to a higher experience-rated schedule allowed by its statute.

Extended programs are financed differently. The Extended Benefit program is financed on a shared basis, half coming either from the state's pooled fund or from experience-rated payments by employers and half from the federal trust fund. Federal Supplemental Benefits are financed entirely by the federal trust funds, using advances from general revenue, while Special Unemployment Assistance is financed out of general revenue.

The Structure of the UI System

Tax and benefit payments depend largely upon the nature of the particular state system. The federal role is felt most directly through the .5-percent federal tax, used partly to finance advances to states that have depleted their funds for regular benefits and for payments on Extended and Federal Supplemental Benefits. The revenues are also used to finance the administrative costs of the states' UI claims operations and their Employment Service functions.

Beyond this, federal intervention in the affairs of state systems is minimal. The provision for a cancellation of 2.7 percentage points of the federal tax is a clear incentive for states wanting to lower taxes to establish an experience-rated system. There are some requirements that workers not be denied benefits until their claims appeals are heard and others that allow all parties engaged in claims determination the right of access to the courts. In general, however, UI consists of a collection of state systems, diverse in all aspects, linked together by coverage rules, a few incentives in the federal law, and the growing acceptance of supplemental federal UI programs financed partly out of the federal tax.

2

Who Pays for UI Benefits and Who Receives Them?

This chapter treats three economic issues. First, how high are taxes, and who pays for the UI system? Although the employer makes the actual contribution in almost all states, the source of the funds may be his customers if he can shift the tax forward; his employees if he shifts it backward; his profits if he cannot shift it; or some combination of these. Second, how large are the benefits relative to the lost income they replace—that is, what is the *replacement rate*? Since one goal of UI policy is income maintenance, we need the best possible estimate of the extent to which incomes are being supported. Third, what is the distribution of benefits by income group? In effect, these three issues involve the impact of UI on the distribution of income and the responsiveness of benefits to changes in income. All changes in UI policy affect income distribution, and estimates of their impact on it should lead to a clearer discussion of their desirability. Here, as in the succeeding chapters, the presentation of factual material will be followed by implications for several specific policy issues that can be analyzed using the discussion in the chapter alone.

Who Bears the UI Tax and How Much Is Paid?

To discover who pays for the UI system and how much, we need to know the impact of the UI tax on wage rates, prices, and profits, both after taxes are initially raised and after the UI system has been in operation for many years. These effects depend to a very large extent on the nature of the UI tax; before we can discover who really pays the tax we must first know who appears to pay it and how taxes vary across states and industries. The average UI tax rate in the country in 1967, a year for which other useful data are available, was 1.61 percent of taxable payrolls. (The base was $3,000 in all but eighteen states.) More interesting, since it permits comparison of states with differing tax bases and average levels of earnings, is the average tax as a fraction of total payrolls (all covered earnings, not simply earnings below the ceiling). For the entire nation in 1967 this averaged only .86 percent, and it has never been above 1.5 percent. Compared with most other taxes—Social Security, profits, personal income, and so forth—this tax generally takes only a small bite out of incomes.

Examination of a number of small industries within broad industry classifications (construction, manufacturing, services, and so forth) is useful for discovering whether firms selling the same products pay similar taxes. Such an examination reveals that most of the differences in average tax rates result from differences in unemployment experience among the broad industry classifications rather than from differences among smaller industries within a broad group. For example, in California in 1967, 68 percent of the variance in average tax rates on taxable wages among thirty-eight industries in six broad groups was due to intergroup differences; in Minnesota in the same year the figure for thirty-nine industries was 51 percent.[1] An analysis of tax rates on total and taxable wages for Michigan in 1968 suggests that if data were available, the California and Minnesota results for tax rates on taxable wages would hold true for tax rates on total wages for the same industries. In short, average tax rates are consistently high in some industries and low in others. Firms selling the same product pay roughly similar UI taxes. This similarity also exists even after we account for benefit payments that vary from industry to industry. Pencavel showed that when the industrial structure was constant the ratio of benefits to taxes appeared

11

to vary more across industries than among states.[2] There is sufficient similarity in experiences within a single large industry to outweigh the effect of interstate differences in benefit and tax structures.

These substantial variations in tax rates and benefit-tax ratios among industries and, to a lesser extent, among labor markets make it hard to discover who eventually pays the UI tax. There is also confusion in the public mind over this basic issue of who pays. A recent book on how to collect UI benefits was subtitled "You worked for it—now collect it."[3] On the other hand, one state Employment Security agency has printed a broadside for posting in covered plants which reads: "Every day many unemployed workers tell us that unemployment insurance is due them 'because they have paid for it.' This is not true in Virginia."[4]

Three different groups could conceivably bear the tax paid by employers: (1) workers, in the form of lower wages; (2) employers, in the form of lower profits; and (3) consumers, including both workers and employers, through higher product prices. Consider first the long-run effects of the imposition of the system of UI benefits and taxes on the U.S. economy in the late 1930s and thus the probable effects of the system today, nearly forty years later. Workers can respond to the imposition of UI by switching employers, and new workers' job choices may differ from those made in the absence of UI. Employers whose profits are especially adversely affected have time to close their plants. Consumers will switch to those products whose prices decline in relative terms after the system is in place. In short, all adjustments occasioned by this institutional change have time to work themselves out.

One implication seems clear: Unless the economy was heavily monopolized beforehand, few excess profits can bear the burden of the tax. If there are only ordinary profits, the employer cannot bear the tax; if he had to do so, he would eventually go out of business. Since in the United States the extent of monopoly profits as a fraction of all profits is not likely to be very large, it is unlikely that employers will bear the tax burden in the long run. Eventually it will be shifted either backward onto workers or forward onto customers.

The eventual split of the tax burden between consumers and workers depends on two sets of factors. The first set is institutional: How much do UI taxes and average benefits differ among firms in the same labor market and among products made in different states but sold in the same product market? We saw that more of the variation in tax rates and benefit-tax ratios is across products than across states. This suggests that consumers will find less variation in UI-induced cost changes among suppliers of a particular product than workers will face among firms in a particular labor market. The second set of factors is behavioral: How readily do workers change employers and location if a rise in UI taxes (benefits) begins to be reflected in wages? and how easily do consumers switch from those products whose prices begin to include UI taxes passed forward by the employer? The greater the ease of moving or switching, the smaller the share of the tax the party must bear. Most likely, only the .5-percent federal tax cannot be escaped by the worker, for the only way for him to avoid employers' attempts to pass it back is to leave the labor force.

We do not know how much of the tax is eventually borne by the system's direct beneficiaries, the workers themselves, and how much is borne by these same beneficiaries (and their employers) in their role as consumers, but some rough estimate is needed in order to discuss most of the issues relevant to UI. Accordingly, we will assume that the burden eventually falls half on consumers and half on workers. Because of the importance of the division of the tax burden between workers and consumers and our imprecise knowledge about it, conclusions based on our assumption will be qualified. We indicate throughout the book how the results may vary depending upon the assumed split between workers and consumers.

If employers do not ultimately pay the tax, why are they so concerned about keeping it down, and why do they lobby so vigorously against UI tax increases? There are several reasons for this behavior that are consistent with our discussion of the burden of the UI tax. First, because of lags in pricing and perception, employers do bear most of the tax during the period after it is initially raised, especially during the first year. Second, large firms having monopoly power are likely to

13

envision reduced profits as a result of the tax, while small employers fear they may be the ones forced to leave the industry when UI taxes rise. Third, employers believe in the "flypaper" theory of taxes—that is, that a tax sticks to the person or firm that actually makes the payment to the tax collector.

Having concluded how the tax is eventually split, we can fairly easily trace its burden on consumers and workers with different incomes and earnings. If we assume that people with different incomes consume similar products, on which the average UI taxes do not differ, we may guess that the consumer's share of the tax is borne in proportion to family income. In effect, this share indirectly taxes a fixed percentage of all consumers' incomes. Because the tax is proportionate, the percentage of total income accruing to each income group is not changed by that part of the tax that is passed forward in the form of higher product prices.

The effect of the burden on workers depends on the limit of the tax base to $4,200. With that limit, low-wage labor pays a larger share of the tax, so that labor's share of the tax is regressive. This conclusion is strengthened if we assume, as is reasonable, that the employer believes low-wage workers are more likely to be laid off and to draw benefits which will raise the experience-rated taxes he must pay. Then he would only hire them at a wage lower than what it would be in the absence of UI, and ipso facto the burden on them would be even greater. So long as both labor and consumers bear part of the tax and the tax base is limited, the tax will be somewhat regressive. The greater the amount borne by labor, the greater the regressiveness of the tax.

The dollars that finance UI benefits are paid by employers to the state. However, the workings of product and labor markets are such that consumers and labor wind up paying the tax through higher prices and lower wages. This implies that policies to expand benefits, which necessarily entail higher taxes, eventually must be paid by people in their roles as consumers and workers. Only in the first few years after taxes are raised can beneficiaries (and other workers for whom the fear of hardships during spells of unemployment is reduced) gain.

Thereafter a policy of higher benefits (and taxes) is financed mainly by shifts in incomes among workers.

How Much Lost Income Is Replaced?

How well do UI benefits cushion (replace) the income losses that result from unemployment? We can use survey data and hypothetical examples to construct estimates of income replacement that answer this question. Five different measures of income replacement can be used. Each is based on a different definition of what constitutes lost income, and each can be useful in judging how well UI maintains incomes.

1. A macroeconomic measure. For several reasons UI replaces only a small fraction of any cyclical decline in aggregate income. First, many job losers are not covered. Second, new entrants to the labor force who become unemployed are not eligible. Third, cyclical declines in income are induced partly by shorter working hours rather than only by complete job loss, which is compensable by UI. Fourth, some UI benefits specifically compensate spells of unemployment resulting from seasonal variations in labor demand. Thus the UI system is implicitly designed not to compensate solely for cyclical declines in incomes.

Given these considerations, it is not surprising that the estimates of replacement of aggregate income losses are as low as they seem. Lester estimates that regular UI benefits replaced an average of 15 percent of the income losses resulting from total and partial unemployment in the four cyclical downturns between 1948 and 1961.[5] Gramlich, using a sample of individuals to calculate the fraction of earnings loss replaced by UI payments in 1971, estimated that only 7 percent of the earnings lost because of shorter hours and partial and total unemployment was replaced among families with a male head of household, and only 18 percent among families with a female head.[6] (Losses replaced for females are greater probably because women are less likely than males to suffer earnings losses through reduced hours or to have their earnings-replacement rate reduced because of limits on maximum benefits.) These figures indicate that the regular UI system is not much of a cushion for declines in income experienced by the economy as a whole.

2. A widely used measure of earnings replacement is the ratio of average weekly benefits paid to average weekly earnings in covered employment. This is a better measure than measure 1, for it recognizes that the UI system is not universal and does not aim to replace earnings losses for all labor-force participants. The ratio has varied between 32 percent and 37 percent since 1947 but varies substantially more across states, as the data in table 2 show. Indeed, in 1974 this ratio ranged from 24 percent in Alaska to 45 percent in Hawaii. This measure is higher where insured-unemployment rates are higher.[7]

The ratio of average benefits paid to average wages in covered employment tells us very little about actual earnings replacement for a UI recipient. The recipient need not be, and most often is not, typical of workers in covered employment. Data for a sample of UI recipients in Ohio show that pre-unemployment earnings of UI recipients in goods-producing industries were 15 percent less than the average earnings of all workers in those industries between 1965 and 1972.[8] In service industries the pre-unemployment earnings of UI recipients were 11 percent less than average. In the aggregate data the results of this difference are reflected in the rise in the ratio of average benefits to covered earnings that has occurred in all postwar recessions. This increase occurs because in a recession proportionately more skilled workers are added to the ranks of the covered unemployed than during a boom. Since benefits are linked to prior earnings, these workers receive higher weekly benefits than do the less-skilled workers, who form the bulk of the insured unemployed during more prosperous times. These composition problems illustrate the faults in this administratively convenient measure, which has often been used for discussing the success (or lack of it) of UI in maintaining incomes. It is not specific to individuals, and it tells us nothing about the fraction of income replaced for a covered employee who experiences unemployment. As such, it does not tell us how well the system succeeds in maintaining the incomes of those whom it is supposed to protect.

The most appropriate measures are those that consider replacement of income for an individual recipient. In measures 3, 4, and 5 we will look at three hypothetical cases of typical individual recipients with differing numbers of dependents in different state systems, and we will then present some sketchy evidence from a survey. We will use as an example a husband-wife family in which the woman does not work and the husband becomes unemployed in 1974. Examples are given for this family with two dependent children, except in the case of Massachusetts. (Because in Massachusetts the existence of dependents' allowances causes substantial differences in replacement among otherwise identical families of different sizes, we also list results for a childless couple.) This hypothetical family has no unearned income other than UI benefits received during total unemployment, and it takes the standard deduction on all income taxes. Most important, we assume that the recipient barely qualifies for the maximum benefit in the state; that is, he has the lowest base-period earnings that would entitle him to the maximum UI benefits paid in the state.

Each hypothetical case represents only the particular state analyzed. Nonetheless, together they are useful in illustrating the differences among various concepts of replacement. The five states used as examples range from very liberal in benefit formulas—Massachusetts and Oregon—to less liberal. The use of a recipient who just qualifies for the maximum benefit guarantees that the ratio of benefits to after-tax earnings will be near the highest possible among the hypothetical cases one could construct. This desire to ensure that there is no underestimation of the true replacement rate is emphasized throughout the calculations by the use of very conservative assumptions on any item that would lower the estimated replacement rate.

3. The simplest measure is the ratio of the worker's total benefits (including dependents' allowances) to the pre-tax earnings he receives when fully employed. These gross replace-

ment rates, based on calculations implicit in each of the five states' statutory provisions, are listed in table 2. In most states the ratio is .50, but in some the formulas are slightly more liberal and the ratio somewhat higher. This measure overstates the true gross replacement, for it ignores delays in filing a UI claim, the one-week waiting period that is noncompensable in the states listed in table 2, and uncompensated weeks of unemployment among exhaustees after benefits run out.

Table 2. Replacement Measures, Selected States, 1974

(1)	State average weekly benefit as fraction of average weekly earnings (2)	Gross replacement benefits/ earnings (3)	Net ratio (incentive effect) (4)	Net ratio (income replacement) (5)
Colorado	.43			
2 children		.60	.66	.60
Massachusetts	.40			
0 children		.50	.56	.52
2 children		.57	.64	.58
New York	.32			
2 children		.50	.56	.52
Oregon	.31			
2 children		.65	.74	.66
South Carolina	.38			
2 children		.50	.55	.49

SOURCES: *Comparison of State Unemployment Insurance Laws*, January 1975; *Handbook of UI Financial Data*, 1938–1970, 1974 supplement; Advisory Council on Intergovernmental Relations, *Federal-State Finances, 1973–1974.*

NOTE: Calculations are described in the text.

Writers on unemployment insurance have long recognized the distinction between *gross* and *net replacement rates*. The latter are defined as ratios of benefits to after-tax earnings and differ from gross rates because UI benefits are not taxed. We construct two such net measures, one indicating the rate at which the net income lost during the most recent week of unemployment is replaced, the other showing replacement over the entire spell of unemployment. The former measures the financial incentive to seek work, while the latter shows how well the UI maintains incomes. The former is based on the tax rate paid on the last dollar of earnings (the marginal tax rate, including federal and state income taxes and the employee's tax payments for Social Security). The latter is based on the average rate at which earnings lost during an entire spell of unemployment would be taxed. With the progressive federal income tax, this rate is less than the marginal rate. The marginal federal tax rates on the earnings of workers in our examples were roughly 16 to 18 percent in 1974, and employees' Social Security (OASDHI) taxes were 5.85 percent of earnings in that year, so the effect of nontaxable benefits will be large.

To derive net replacement correctly, we need to use a broad definition of income, not just the wages on which the gross replacement rate is based. Even if we ignore lost quarters of coverage for Social Security benefits, the unemployed worker in nearly all cases soon loses his health insurance, his employer's pension contributions, and his seniority rights (if his layoff is permanent). In 1974 nonwage labor income other than employers' social-insurance contributions was 6.8 percent of wages. A survey of large employers reported that pension and insurance costs were 10.5 percent of total payroll. [9] These figures probably understate the true value of some fringes, for the cost to the worker of buying the benefit in the market (health insurance premiums, for example) greatly exceeds the cost to his employer of providing it. Nonetheless, the replacement rates that reflect marginal and average income losses, measures 4 and 5, add only an amount equaling 10 percent of pre-tax wages to the estimate of lost income during unemployment. Further, they subtract from gross income 1.5 percent, a rough reflection of the monetary costs of travel to work—bus or train fare, gasoline, and so forth.

Another consideration arises from the need to account for inflation. The usual 50-percent gross replacement rate, measure 3, compares benefits to base-period earnings. Given the laws in most (thirty-five) states, the average month in the base period is at least nine months before the worker files his UI claim. With more rapid wage inflation, the wage obtained while the worker is employed and the wage just prior to layoff are higher than the average wage in the base period. Thus in 1974, for example, when the average annual rate of wage inflation was 8.5 percent, the average wage received just before the worker's layoff probably differed from his average base-period wages by at least 6 percent. This correction factor is also applied to derive measures 4 and 5.

A final modification to measure 3 is required to account for the fact that during the noncompensable waiting period the claimant receives no benefits in the five states used in our examples. The replacement rate for that week is zero. Accordingly, the average replacement rate for an entire spell of unemployment for the beneficiary is slightly less than the replacement rate for the period beginning after the first week. This does not affect the calculation of the possible incentive effects, since they are based on an additional week unemployed, presumably some weeks after the waiting period.

4. Measure 4, the incentive measure based on marginal tax rates, is generally slightly higher than gross replacement. The net benefits for an unemployed husband with two children of remaining unemployed an additional week instead of taking a job yielding a net income of $100 per week range from $55 per week in South Carolina to $74 per week in Oregon. (Furthermore, evidence produced by Mills suggests that accounting for other transfer payments would raise these replacement rates only very slightly.)[10] These rates are fairly substantial, but they do suggest the existence of a financial incentive to seek work. It should be remembered that (1) they are based on conservative assumptions about the value of fringe benefits; (2) because our hypothetical families qualify (just barely) for the maximum benefit, the difference between gross and net replacement rates for them will be larger than average (since their tax rates are higher than those of the average UI claimant); and (3) they reflect the relative values of another week of unemployment compared with a week of employment. They do not measure net income replaced.

5. Measure 5 in table 2 reflects the replacement of net income for the hypothetical families. It makes the appropriate

additions that we have discussed, calculates net income based on average tax rates, and accounts for the waiting period. Even so, it overstates the average replacement rate by ignoring income lost due to delays in filing UI claims and unreplaced income after a worker has exhausted his UI benefits. In all cases the net replacement rates are remarkably close to the gross replacement rates (measure 3) upon which they are based. The gross rates ranged from .50 to .65, the net rates from .49 to .66. Adding lost fringe benefits and accounting for wage inflation and the waiting period nearly exactly offset the effects of accounting for the nontaxation of UI benefits.

A recent survey of 1,757 exhaustees in 1974–75 provides the first piece of hard evidence on actual replacement adjusted for taxes.[11] In a sample for eight metropolitan areas around the country the average value of a measure like measure 4, based on earnings in the week prior to unemployment, was .54. (Inclusion of work-related expenses raised this figure only slightly.) This figure varied little with race but was somewhat higher among exhaustees who had no children (partly because tax rates are higher for them). Its highest value, .75, was for female exhaustees with husbands, probably because their spouses' earnings placed them in higher tax brackets and because they were less likely to be affected by state benefit maxima. If we had data based on measure 5, they would result in estimates below .54 (or .75), since they would include income lost during the waiting period and would be based on the (lower) average tax rates.

The net ratios suggest that the true replacement rate may be somewhat higher than the replacement indicated by a measure that compares average benefits with average earnings of covered employees (measure 2). Net income replacement, not gross income replaced, is clearly the correct measure to consider when trying to evaluate how well the UI system protects the purchasing power, and thus the economic well-being, of its beneficiaries. The evidence is fairly strong that on the average, slightly more than half of the beneficiaries' net compensation is replaced by UI benefits. As an income-maintenance policy UI succeeds in replacing much of the income lost by those individuals at whom the program is targeted. It does, though, retain an incentive for the recipient to seek work.

Table 3. Characteristics of the Unemployed (Survey) and the Insured Unemployed (State Programs), March 1973 and March 1975 (in percent)

	March 1973		March 1975	
	Unem-ployed (Survey)	Insured unem-ployed	Unem-ployed (Survey)	Insured unem-ployed
White	80.4	86.0	82.2	84.6
Age:				
< 25	46.8	17.6	43.5	24.0
25–54	43.8	60.5	47.5	62.3
55 +	9.4	21.9	9.0	13.7
Females	43.9	38.0	41.5	33.8

SOURCES: Bureau of Labor Statistics, *Employment and Earnings*, April 1973, April 1975; *Unemployment Insurance Statistics*, May 1974, May 1975.

Who Receives UI Benefits?

The percentage distribution of UI beneficiaries by demographic group is conditioned both by the incidence of unemployment and by the rules determining eligibility for benefits. Table 3 presents distributions of unemployed workers by demographic group—age, sex, and race. The figures are given for March 1973 and March 1975 to illustrate the changes that occurred in these distributions as the economy moved from boom to recession. As one would expect, given the eligibility requirements for UI, the representation of youths in the distribution of insured unemployed is low compared with their representation among the unemployed as defined in the monthly household survey (Current Population Survey). For example, in March 1973, 46.8 percent of the unemployed in the household survey were less than twenty-five years old, while only 17.6 percent of the insured unemployed were. More detailed data indicate that this is true for both sexes and for both whites and nonwhites, although especially for nonwhites. Older workers are disproportionately represented in the count of insured unemployed compared with estimates of their unemployment based on the household survey. Finally, women represent a smaller fraction of the insured unemployed than they do in the household survey.

Some interesting changes occurred in the relative distributions of unemployed between March 1973 and March 1975. While the distribution of unemployment by age in the household survey changed only slightly between the two periods, the worsening economic conditions produced a substantially younger set of UI beneficiaries. No sharp changes are observed in the relative distribution of unemployment between whites and nonwhites or between males and females. Some care is required in interpreting these changes, however, because the introduction of Federal Supplemental Benefits could have induced changes in the distribution of insured unemployed even under state programs in March 1975. We cannot unequivocally attribute the observed change in the age distribution of beneficiaries to changing economic conditions, although one must believe that the move from a labor market with 5 percent civilian unemployment to one with 8.7 percent is responsible.

The different definitions of unemployment in the household survey and in the count of claimants of UI benefits ensure that the distributions of household and insured unemployed will differ. While these discrepancies at first glance may appear to result from abuse of UI benefits, they occur legitimately within the regulations of the state UI systems. Six cases are conceivable: (1) An individual may be receiving UI benefits yet mistakenly report himself as out of the labor force when confronted with the questions in the household survey. (2) He may be receiving benefits (that is, he may be among the insured unemployed) yet report himself as employed if he is only partially employed and his state allows partial UI benefits. (3) He may report himself as unemployed in the household survey yet not be receiving UI benefits. This case is most common, for it typifies new entrants to the labor force and others who are ineligible for benefits. The other three cases (as defined by the survey)—receiving benefits while unemployed; not receiving benefits while employed; and not receiving benefits while out of the labor force—do not excite much controversy.

23

The data show that benefits are paid to the more mature unemployed worker, to men relatively more than women, and to whites relatively more than nonwhites. In no sense do these results, implicit in the comparison of distributions of unemployment from table 3, reflect discrimination in the payment of UI benefits. Disparities arise partly from different definitions of unemployment between the commonly used survey data and the count of insured unemployed. Definitions of insured unemployment stem from a set of rules for eligibility and coverage established through the political process at the federal and state levels.

The demographic distribution of UI claimants tells us little about the distribution of UI benefits by demographic group, income class, or earnings category. Benefit amounts differ systematically between youthful and mature recipients, males and females, and nonwhites and whites. Furthermore, benefit amounts may be systematically related to other family income. Recipients qualifying for the maximum may be those whose spouses have higher earnings or who, as a result of higher earnings over their working lives, have accumulated some assets and thus have higher unearned incomes than do other UI recipients.

The only available information on incomes is based on data calculated by Feldstein using a 1966 survey adjusted to 1970 prices.[12] Income is defined broadly to include the items ordinarily counted as income as well as the value of services from owner-occupied housing, tax-exempt interest, accrued capital gains, and employer-paid fringe benefits. The data show that the 54 percent of families with adjusted incomes between $5,000 and $20,000 included 68 percent of UI beneficiaries. The poorest 28 percent of families included 18 percent of all beneficiaries, while the richest 18 percent included only 14 percent. In this sample it appears that families whose members receive UI benefits fall disproportionately in the income classes between $5,000 and $20,000. If there were no problems of systematic bias in the respondents' answers about whether they received any UI benefits, this would suggest that those individuals helped by the program are predominantly between the 30th and 80th percentiles of all families, ranked by family income. In fact, there was substantial underreporting of UI benefits in the survey on which this table is based. It is likely that its extent was greater among low-income families so that the results probably understate somewhat the extent to which UI benefits aid low-income families.

These data tell us only which families, by income class, receive benefits, not how much. The calculations also show, though, that the lowest 53 percent of families (with adjusted family incomes below $10,000) received 48 percent of all dollars paid as UI benefits. This contrasts sharply with estimates of inequality in the distribution of all income in the original survey. The original data show that the lowest 60 percent of families received only 29 percent of the aggregate adjusted income in 1966.[13] The distribution of adjusted incomes including UI benefits is thus substantially more equal than the distribution without them.

UI recipients do not belong chiefly to the population of families below the poverty line, nor do they belong to the upper middle class. Given the requirements for eligibility and coverage, this finding should not be too surprising. We have also seen that the distribution of UI benefits differs greatly from the distribution of total money incomes. A much larger fraction of total benefits than of total money income goes to persons in families whose incomes are below the median family income. UI benefits thus tend to equalize the distribution of after-tax incomes in the United States. This also is not surprising, for lower-wage workers have more and longer spells of unemployment, and benefit maxima affect mainly workers in higher-income families.

We have compared the distributions of UI benefits and family incomes, but the program is geared to individuals' labor-market experiences. Along with dependents' allowances, it is these labor-market experiences that determine the size of recipients' benefits. We have no data on the distribution of UI benefits by earnings class of individuals in the labor force, a measure that is more appropriate, given the program's focus on the individual worker. (But it is clearly less appropriate for examining the overall distributional effects of the program because the family is the basic consuming unit. Comparisons by family income are also more useful for considering net replacement rates, since tax rates are based in most tax returns on family incomes rather than individual incomes.) Data for Ohio imply that the median beneficiary's earnings when he works are 15 percent below those of the median worker in covered employment,[14] which corroborates the finding that benefits increase equality in the income distribution.

Any conclusions about the net impact of unemployment insurance—both benefits and taxes—on the distribution of income are necessarily quite tentative. We can be fairly sure that benefits go disproportionately more to people in the middle of the income distribution or slightly below the middle and that they equalize the distribution of income. However, the burden of the tax by income class depends on how it is split between workers and consumers. Our assumption of an even split implies that the tax is slightly regressive, for the ceiling on the tax base makes the burden on low-wage labor disproportionately heavy, and the burden on consumers is proportionate across income groups. Taking the impacts of taxes and benefits together, we can conclude that the net impact of UI is probably small. There is little evidence that UI was intended to redistribute incomes, and in fact it does not appear to do so.

Specific Policy Issues

Although many of the areas for which this discussion has important implications require further consideration, several can be analyzed in light of the economic issues discussed thus far. First among these is the question of *dependents' allowances*. These are provided in only eleven states (a number that has changed little in the last twenty years). Only 36 percent of the beneficiaries in those states received dependents' allowances in fiscal 1974. These beneficiaries comprised 7.8 percent of all eligible claimants in the nation, but the dependents' allowances constituted only 1.3 percent of benefits paid under all state programs. These payments clearly are not of major importance in the total UI program, but they do raise a policy question: Should claimants whose pre-unemployment experiences are identical receive different total benefit amounts solely because they happen to differ in number of dependent children or marital status? (In the case of dependent spouses the issue is less important, since only two states, Connecticut and Pennsylvania, automatically qualify spouses for allowances, while five other states place a ceiling on their earnings.)

A federal requirement that induces states to cease providing dependents' allowances should be introduced if other federal standards become law. UI should not discriminate among potential beneficiaries whose employment and unemployment experiences are the same. To do so denies equity within the context of the considerations that currently govern benefit determination, namely, the claimant's previous work history. Only if one views the program as an income transfer based on need is there a justification for dependents' allowances. Such a view has several difficulties: (1) Once the door to the needs criterion is opened, there is no argument against the encroachment of still further needs considerations. This undermines the program's broad political appeal—the feeling that it compensates the victims of industrial fluctuations—and increases its identification in the public mind with what are purely welfare programs; (2) it implicitly favors families that through their own choice have more children than others or determine that one spouse will work at home rather than in the market; and (3) it forces firms, which initially bear the costs of higher UI taxes, to bear greater costs for those workers with more dependents. This affects labor demand, for the relative costs of employing different workers are changed. Thus a needs-based view, even if adopted for only the relatively minor issue of dependents' allowances, may not be costless in terms of its economic effect.

Taxation of UI benefits is a sharp departure from the program's traditions, although some foreign UI systems do pay taxable benefits. Since government transfers to individuals are exempted from the income tax, taxing UI benefits would require revision of the entire tax code. Despite the political difficulties, such a change is worth considering on economic grounds. If this

27

change were made, political imperatives would require increasing before-tax benefits for most recipients so that recipients as a group would be kept equally well-off.

The best argument for taxing UI benefits is that of equity broadly based: Two eligible claimants with identical work experiences but different wages while employed receive benefits that produce unequal net replacement rates. Recipients with higher earnings who still receive less than the maximum benefit have proportionately more of their net income loss replaced. This is not the desired result of a system that at least partly intends to treat beneficiaries in a way commensurate with their labor-market experience, and it results from the growth in the progressive personal income tax since the inception of the UI program. Taxation of benefits would ensure that the net wage loss of beneficiaries in different tax brackets was proportional.

A problem of internal consistency arises when we consider the implications for equity within the narrow context of the UI system alone. The system now seeks to treat recipients with identical employment experiences as equals. However, if Jones receives interest income while Smith receives none, or if Jones's wife works, equal benefit payments will replace more of Jones's net-earnings loss if the benefits are not taxed (since more of Jones's earnings would be taxed away by the progressive income tax). Taxing benefits equalizes the replacement of their lost net earnings, but it leads to a smaller replacement of gross earnings for Jones. However, this should not disturb those who wish to retain those provisions that resemble a needs-based transfer program, for taxing benefits avoids giving the greatest aid to those unemployed who least need it.

Considerations of income from all sources dictate the taxing of UI benefits. The broad equity considerations appear sufficient to outweigh the lack of consistency in program construction implicit in using a broad definition of income rather than merely referring to labor-market experience, so that taxation of benefits appears desirable.

In 1975 *maximum benefits* were 60 percent or more of the state average weekly wage in only fifteen states. Workers earning slightly more than the state average wage in the base period thus received a gross replacement rate of less than 50 percent in many states, and the rate declines as base-period earnings rise. It is not surprising that in 1972, for example, 44 percent of claimants nationwide were eligible for maximum benefits. As early as 1955 the Eisenhower administration proposed that benefit maxima be raised so that "a great majority" of beneficiaries would not have their weekly benefits limited by the maximum benefits. The same principle is implicit in recent federal proposals for a uniform benefit maximum equal to two thirds or three quarters of the state average weekly wage.[15]

Before any federally mandated increase could be made acceptable politically, the tax base would need to be raised. Only then would it appear that individuals with high earnings who benefited from increased benefit maxima were bearing a proportionate share of the burden of financing the system. Assuming this were accomplished—policy on the tax base is discussed in chapter 4—how high should the ceiling on benefits be? Two points lead to the conclusion that there should be no ceiling if benefits are taxed. First, endless argument over the appropriate fraction of beneficiaries to receive a gross replacement rate of 50 percent would be removed. Use of any particular figure for a benefit maximum arbitrarily restricts benefits for some high-wage beneficiaries, and there is no justification for making the fraction to receive 50 percent gross replacement "a great majority," 65 percent, 75 percent, or even 90 percent. Second, excluding highly paid beneficiaries from receipt of a gross replacement rate of 50 percent of their wage loss introduces needs-related considerations into the program.

Should the policy of *employee contributions* to state UI funds, now followed in three states, be expanded to the entire system? Taxation of employees to cover a state's noncharged benefits is probably within the political realm of possibility. Implementation could occur on the state or federal level. Assuming there is no change in the tax base, placing some of the burden directly on workers would initially lower taxes paid by employers. Employment demand would increase, which would increase the number of jobs available. It is likely, however, that the part of UI taxes common to all employers (the federal tax) is eventually borne mostly by workers. Natural labor-market adjustments would probably bring the economy back to where it was before the change, unless other alterations in the structure of UI were also effected. The best arguments for this change are that it would give the appearance of increasing the insurance nature of the program and would enable experience rating to be made more perfect (see chapter 4). It would serve to alter employees' perceptions about the program by increasing the steady worker's sense of participation in the UI system. Furthermore, it well might mollify employers who feel that the worker should pay (presumably directly) some part of the system's costs. Although the economic effects will probably be small, the political benefits could be substantial, and these in turn could induce greater beneficial changes in the behavior of workers and employers than past observations would lead one to expect.

3

The UI System and the Worker

According to Arthur Burns, chairman of the Federal Reserve Board, net replacement rates varying between one half and two thirds "may be blunting incentives to work."[1] Employer groups, some academic economists, and various administration statements have echoed his view. We examine in this chapter whether the unemployment rate is higher because of disincentives to workers than it would be in the absence of the UI program, and if so, by how much. The number of unemployed at any time depends on the size of the labor force, the number of spells of unemployment experienced by labor-force participants, and the average duration of those spells. If we assume for the moment that UI produces no change in the number of spells of unemployment per person in the labor force, its effects on unemployment and the unemployment rate depend on the answers to two separate questions: (1) Does it increase the duration of spells of unemployment? (2) Does it change the size of the labor force? Any effect must be expressed through these two mechanisms (if the number of spells does not vary). Since the effect of UI on the number of spells operates chiefly through employers' demands for labor, this aspect will be reserved for discussion in chapter 4, and the total effect on unemployment will be discussed in chapter 6.

31

Two economic-policy questions are implicit in the analysis of the UI system's effect on the labor market. First, does the system produce a waste of real resources by inducing individuals to substitute extra unemployment that partly can be used as leisure for time spent in productive employment in the market? Second, have changes in the UI system over the past twenty-five years affected the usefulness of the aggregate unemployment rate as an indicator for macroeconomic policy? If, for example, these changes have induced more workers to spend more time unemployed, a 6-percent unemployment rate would denote a tighter labor market today than it did twenty-five years ago. And this would suggest the need to revise our views about what constitutes low unemployment.

UI and the Duration of Unemployment

Doubling the average duration of spells of unemployment while holding the labor force and number of spells constant doubles the insured-unemployment rate. If the UI system affects the duration of completed spells of unemployment, we may conclude that insured unemployment varies in proportion to the change in duration induced by the program. Between 1947 and 1974 the average duration of weeks of insured unemployment for which the individual received benefits (*benefit-weeks*) ranged from 10.1 to 14.8. The lower figure was reached during the Korean War, while the highest average duration occurred during the 1958 recession. Duration clearly rises as the demand for labor falls. The relative lack of variation over time in the national average masks substantial variation in average duration among states in any year. The national average in 1974 was 12.7 weeks, but state averages ranged from 7.5 in New Hampshire and North Carolina to 16.8 in Alaska and 19.1 in the District of Columbia. Within any state the range is obviously greater still, usually ranging from one week to the maximum potential duration under the state's system.

The effect of changes in benefit amounts and potential duration on the measures of duration of unemployment can be considered from the point of view of a UI recipient who has already been receiving regular benefits for some weeks. Examining his behavior in this context outlines the general way that UI affects the behavior of the unemployed and shows how changes in UI policy parameters can affect unemployment. The recipient weighs the choice between taking a job and remaining unemployed (and drawing benefits) yet another week. A higher benefit amount or greater potential duration has two effects. The first results from the lower cost of an additional week of unemployment. The loss from another week of unemployment is the excess of the net wage on the job over the weekly UI benefit amount. If the weekly benefit is raised, workers will be more likely to stay unemployed an additional week, since the lost income from doing so is lower. (The replacement rate that best represents this is based on measure 4, the net replacement rate that ignores the wages lost during the noncompensable waiting period.) This first (substitution) effect of increased benefits will always lead the worker to spend more time unemployed.

The second effect occurs because UI benefits raise the amount of resources at the unemployed worker's command and so enable him to buy more of all those goods he wishes to consume. Since people presumably enjoy leisure, this effect can work to increase the chance that the UI beneficiary will spend another week unemployed. On the other hand, higher benefits enable the recipient to buy more resources necessary for his job-search activities. Depending upon his tastes for leisure versus work and the potential productivity of the additional resources devoted to searching for work, the net result of this second (income) effect can be either to increase or decrease the likelihood that the beneficiary will remain unemployed another week. Indeed, if it is negative (that is, if his likelihood of remaining unemployed drops), it is even possible, although not likely, that it can outweigh the positive substitution effect, so that higher weekly benefits will decrease the time spent unemployed.

The effects of increased potential duration are likely to be quite different. A higher weekly benefit affects all recipients' choices about remaining unemployed; its results immediately change the relative value of another week of unemployment for all beneficiaries, regardless of how long they have been unemployed. An increase in the potential duration of benefits affects more strongly the choices of those workers who are nearing the point when their entitlement would otherwise be exhausted. Since relatively few recipients reach this stage except in a recession, extensions of potential duration will probably affect fewer workers than will increases in weekly benefits.

The extent of both effects of changed benefit amounts depends upon the state of the labor market. When unemployment is unusually high, it is partly because the duration of spells of unemployment is long. The lack of available jobs forces workers to spend more time at leisure than when labor-market conditions are better. Accordingly, the substitution effect of increased weekly benefits is smaller. Since the recipients are more likely to be bored staying at home, additional UI benefits will have little chance of deterring them from taking a job should one become available. Furthermore, the income effect is more likely to be negative. Because of the depletion of funds that accompanies the greater duration of unemployment in bad times, UI recipients will be more likely to use the increased benefits to look for work. For both reasons, then, any detrimental effect of increased UI benefits on the duration of unemployment will be less than in good times. However, because in a recession the duration of spells of unemployment is longer regardless of the nature of the UI program, and because more people are nearing exhaustion of their benefits then, increases in maximum potential duration may produce more of an effect on average duration than at other times.

Of all the economic issues analyzed in this book, most extensively analyzed by economists, especially since 1973, has been the effect of UI on the duration of unemployment. We examine here the effects of changes in weekly benefits and potential duration on recipients' benefit-weeks, usually in a calendar year, or on their actual weeks of unemployment, recognizing that the age-sex composition of the unemployed is held constant in most studies. The effect on actual weeks of unemployment is clearly more important for estimating the labor-market impact of UI, but many studies use only data on benefit-weeks.

Table 4. Studies of the Effects of UI Benefits on the Duration of Unemployment

Study	Data	Effect on weeks of unemployment	Study	Data	Effect on weeks on unemployment
Burgess and Kingston (1974)	Boston, Bay Area, Phoenix, 1969–70		Felder (1975)	Denver, 1970	
	Males	.01		Males	1.4
	Females	-.04		Females	1.4
Chapin (1971)	All states, 1962–67	.46	Hanna et al. (1975)	Nevada, 1969–72	1.0
Classen (1975)	Pennsylvania, 1967–68	1.1	Holen (1976)	Boston, Bay Area, Phoenix, 1969–70	.60
Crosslin (1975)	St. Louis, 1971–73	-.09	Lininger (1963)	Michigan, 1955	.06
	Cleveland, 1970	-.05	Marston (1975)	Based on Detroit, 1969	.23–.62
Ehrenberg and Oaxaca (1976)	Nationwide		Schmidt (1974)	Nationwide, 1966	1.6
	Males		Wandner (1975)	All states	
	Aged 45–59, 1966–67	1.5		1966–69	.53
	Aged 14–24, 1966–69	.2		1959–62	.03
	Females				
	Aged 30–44, 1968–71	.3			
	Aged 14–24, 1967–70	.5			

Table 4 summarizes the available studies of the effects of UI benefits on the duration of unemployment in the United States. In order to make the studies comparable, we calculate the effect on duration of either a 10-percentage-point increase in the ratio of weekly benefits to the average weekly wage or a $10 increase in weekly benefits. (The second choice was made only in the studies by Classen, Felder, and Holen, in which the nature of the empirical work made it impossible to use the first measure. Since the average weekly wage in covered employment was roughly $100 in the late 1960s and early 1970s, and since the gross replacement rate [measure 3] is roughly 50 percent, these two calculations are roughly equivalent.) The reader should bear in mind that the estimated effects on duration are based on calculations that assume nothing else changes. We pose the following questions: How much greater would the average duration of claims have been in the sample period and place if benefits had been higher but nothing else had been altered? To what extent do higher UI benefits contribute to longer spells of unemployment among those who lose their jobs?

A quick perusal of the estimated effects presented in table 4 could lead to the conclusion that the studies tell us nothing. The numbers range from less than zero (a greater benefit amount decreases average duration!) to 1.6, indicating that a 10-percentage-point rise in weekly benefits increases duration by 1.6 weeks. But one cannot simply take an average of the studies' results and conclude that it is the best estimate available. The results of the Chapin and Wandner studies are somewhat suspect, since they use data on states that might produce errors in estimates because of the definitional relationship between statewide unemployment rates and the average duration in the state. Both the Crosslin and the Burgess and Kingston studies use data on claimants interviewed as part of a special project; their results may be biased because of this extra attention. (Holen used these same data plus additional claimants who were not interviewed and found very different effects.)

The studies of Classen, Felder, and Hanna et al. use data on individuals within a state, and their results are remarkably close, considering that they use different states and different time periods. Each suggests that a 10-percentage-point increase in the gross replacement rate (measure 3) leads to roughly a one-week increase in benefit-weeks paid. Marston's figures are much lower, but this may be because they reflect the actual duration of unemployment—the more interesting measure—whereas Classen and Hanna et al. measure the effect on benefit-weeks. Higher weekly benefits encourage more potential claimants to file their initial claims immediately after becoming unemployed. Thus, part of the measured increase in benefit-weeks is produced by shorter filing delays, so that the increase in the duration of all spells of unemployment is probably less than the increase in benefit-weeks. The Lininger results are difficult to explain, but they may reflect the unsurprising findings reported by Classen and by Ehrenberg and Oaxaca that the duration of unemployment of workers on recall is affected by changes in weekly benefits much less than is that of job changers. Lininger's results may be due to the unusually large fraction of UI recipients in Michigan on recall to the auto industry.

From this large and rapidly expanding literature the best estimate—if one chooses a single figure—is that a 10-percentage-point increase in the gross replacement rate (measure 3) leads to an increase in the duration of insured unemployment of about half a week when labor markets are tight. This is not an exact figure, but it does appear that there is some effect, certainly above zero and probably less than one week. A more precise estimate awaits a study that embodies the best features of all those mentioned in table 4.

Although there is no empirical evidence either way, it is likely that UI induces shorter spells of unemployment among reentrants and new labor-force entrants (the opposite of its effects on job losers). This effect occurs because the existence of UI induces them to take jobs more quickly in order to qualify for benefits in their next spell of unemployment. We ignore it in our calculations later in this chapter, which means that we are (probably slightly) overestimating the impact of UI on total unemployment.

Few of the studies estimate the effects of UI on duration at different points in the business cycle, and most are based at least partly on the low-unemployment years 1965–69. However,

Wandner does show that the effect of benefits on average duration was smaller in the high-unemployment years 1959–62 than in 1966–69, and he uses the more correct average benefit-weeks per spell of unemployment rather than the more commonly used measure of average benefit-weeks during a year. Although this empirical evidence is weak, especially given Wandner's use of data on state averages, it is very likely that these effects are much smaller, perhaps even zero, when the civilian unemployment rate is above 6 percent. UI benefits do increase the duration of spells of unemployment among the insured unemployed, but the effect is probably small when there are few job vacancies.

Several of the studies listed in table 4 examined the effect of increased potential duration on the average duration of spells of unemployment. While the results are sparse, they tend to support the belief that the effect of increased potential duration on the number of weeks that an individual draws benefits increases when unemployment is high. Burgess and Kingston, using data from 1969–70, find no effect for males and only a .14-week increase for females for a one-week increase in potential duration. Crosslin, using data from 1971–73, finds a .62-week increase in average duration; and Hanna et al., using data from 1969–72, find a .91-week increase when potential duration is raised by one week.

An interesting corroboration of the studies in table 4 is provided by Mackay and Reid.[2] They sampled laid-off British factory workers and calculated their responses both to unemployment benefits (paid each week for up to twenty-six weeks) and to the payment received all at once when the worker was first laid off. The response of duration was .84 weeks per 10-percentage-point increase in replacement, similar to that found in the most careful U.S. studies. More interesting is the fact that the effect of the initial payment on duration was essentially zero. To produce the same increase in duration generated by a 10-percentage-point (£ 2) increase in the weekly replacement rate, the initial payment would need to be increased by £ 168 (seven times the extra transfer paid to the average worker during his entire spell of unemployment). The initial payment produces a pure income effect. Because it is given all at once, it affects only the resources at the recipient's command, not the cost of remaining unemployed another week. The result supports the conjecture that the income effect will be smaller than the substitution effect and adds some validity to our economic analysis of the effects of UI benefits on workers' behavior. It also suggests one way that income can be transferred to beneficiaries without affecting substantially the length of their spells of unemployment.

Job Search and Its Effect on Post-unemployment Earnings

How is the extra half week of unemployment produced by each extra ten percentage points of earnings replacement used by the insured unemployed? Is the time used to search for and find better (more stable and higher paying) employment, or is it used as leisure? If the former, the cost of the UI system can be viewed as a useful investment that produces higher earnings when the worker becomes reemployed. If the latter, from society's standpoint the costs are mostly wasted; their only output is more time spent by the unemployed at leisure.

The impact of UI can be considered indirectly, in terms of its effects on search behavior, or directly, in terms of its ultimate effects on earnings in the recipient's next job. The indirect approach has substantial initial appeal. If subsequent employment, especially for those not on temporary layoff, is to result in higher wages for the average recipient (abstracting from inflation), UI must provide the chance for more, or more fruitful, contacts between him and potential employers. Unfortunately, while many studies have examined job-seeking behavior, the only evidence relating it to UI claimant status is that claimants have fewer problems than other unemployed workers in finding transportation to look for work.[3] We also know that registration with the Employment Service ipso facto provides the claimant with more opportunities for potential contacts with employers. If using the Employment Service is an efficient method of search, and if claimants do not substitute registration there for other methods of search, the UI system can provide more contacts with employers and thus aid in job seeking.

A modification of the direct approach is to consider the effect of UI benefits on the wage the unemployed worker seeks in the jobs offered to him. Much research has examined this concept, and we know that the wage sought falls as the duration of unemployment lengthens. However, only Katz has examined how its rate of decline is affected by higher UI benefits.[4] He finds that during each month of unemployment it falls 2 percent more rapidly among UI beneficiaries than among nonclaimants, who are otherwise similar, but that immediately after the spell of unemployment begins it is 18 percent higher among UI recipients. Since the average duration of unemployment is far below nine months, if other things are equal we can conclude that UI benefits raise the level of the wage unemployed workers are willing to accept on subsequent jobs. To the extent that UI beneficiaries engage in as much useful search activity per week as others (during their slightly longer spells of unemployment), this suggests that the wage they receive on their post-unemployment job can exceed that received by individuals who do not draw benefits.

The direct approach masks the entire process of job seeking and the consequent revision of the wage sought by the unemployed worker. By ignoring the intermediate steps, however, it can enable us to draw conclusions about the net effect of longer unemployment on subsequent earnings. Five of the studies on the duration of insured unemployment listed in table 4 provide evidence on this. The findings can be considered in conjunction with those on the effects of higher benefits on duration. The result is a very mixed picture indeed. Burgess and Kingston find no effect on duration but find immense (24 and 14 percent for males and females, respectively) increases in weekly wages over what the claimant received before he filed his initial claim.[5] This implies, not an increase in the time spent unemployed, but rather that the period of unemployment is used much more intensively in highly productive job search. Holen, using some of the same data, finds a significant effect on duration and effects on post-unemployment earnings ranging from 6 to 8 percent in the cities she used.[6] Ehrenberg and Oaxaca and Schmidt produce substantial effects on duration and find moderate (between 1.5 and 7 percent) increases in wages among adult claimants.[7] Classen finds essentially no effect on post-unemployment wages but a substantial increase in the duration of unemployment.[8] All five studies abstract from earnings gains resulting from inflation.

This diversity of results precludes specific conclusions about how the extra time spent unemployed is used. Greater UI benefits do appear to induce a longer duration of unemployment—roughly on the order of .5 weeks for each 10-percentage-point increase in benefits when the labor market is tight. Whether this extra time is used as leisure or as productive search leading to greater earnings cannot be inferred from existing studies. At this time we simply do not know whether UI is succeeding as a policy designed to allow the unemployed a chance to find better jobs than they would otherwise obtain.

Exhaustions, Potential Duration, and Insured Unemployment

A beneficiary exhausts his regular benefits (becomes an exhaustee) if he is still unemployed when his entitlement to regular state benefits ceases. The actual duration of his weeks of insured unemployment then equals his potential duration. Unless an extended program is in effect, he must rely on alternative means of support if he cannot find a job. We examine here the number of workers who exhaust benefits (Extended Benefits, not just the shorter entitlement to regular state benefits); how exhaustions vary cyclically across states and by demographic group; what effect differences in potential duration have on measured insured unemployment, and how these effects are important for policy analysis.

An *exhaustion rate* is defined as the percentage of exhaustees among those beneficiaries whose initial claims were filed six months before a given month. (The six-month [twenty-six-week] lag corresponds increasingly closely to the average potential duration of regular state benefits.) In the United States as a whole the exhaustion rate varied between roughly 20 percent and 31 percent between 1955 and 1974; it rose during recessions and fell during booms. Preliminary data show that the previous high exhaustion rate was exceeded in 1975. The exhaustion rate of regular benefits was 47 percent, but many of these exhaustees received Extended or Federal Supplemental Benefit payments that lasted until they found work.

Exhaustion rates differ among states for two major reasons. First, because the degree of labor-market tightness varies, there will be differences in the ease with which beneficiaries can either find a new job or become reemployed in their previous job. The second and more interesting reason is the difference among states in the potential duration of benefits available to UI claimants. Where potential duration is longer, exhaustion rates will be lower, for beneficiaries have more time to become reemployed before their regular entitlement is used up. A comparison of two of the states we use as examples, New York and South Carolina, illustrates this vividly. In New York, where all beneficiaries are entitled to the uniform potential duration of twenty-six weeks, exhaustion rates are generally below those of South Carolina, where potential duration varies with base-period earnings up to a maximum potential duration of twenty-six weeks. Between 1955 and 1974, even though the insured unemployment rate in New York was never less than that in South Carolina, the exhaustion rate in New York was always lower.

Except in those states with uniform potential duration, we find that exhaustions occur among those claimants with below-average potential duration of benefits. In South Carolina and other states where potential duration is variable, in all years average potential (and thus actual) duration of exhaustees' benefits was one to two weeks below the average potential duration for all claimants. Exhaustees are more likely to be those whose base-period employment and earnings are below those of the average claimant and whose potential duration of benefits is thus below average. A study in ten states in May 1975 showed exhaustees to be comprised disproportionately of black and female claimants, with a slightly less than proportional representation of claimants 22–44 years old.[9] Given the statutory linkage of potential duration to base-period employment and earnings in states with variable potential duration, and given the looser labor-force attachment of blacks, women, and very young and older workers, the pattern of exhaustions by age, race, and sex is predictable.

The appropriate measure of exhaustions to indicate the fraction of the target population no longer protected by the UI program is the exhaustion rate of all benefits—before 1970, regular state benefits alone; after 1970, Extended Benefits if they were operative in the state; and since March 1975, Federal Supplemental Benefits up through a maximum of sixty-five weeks. An exhaustion rate based on total benefits clearly will be lower than one based on regular benefits. Some exhaustees of regular benefits will become reemployed before their additional entitlement expires. In New York, for example, paying UI benefits for weeks 27–39 of unemployment reduced the fraction exhausting by about one third (from 24.7 to 14.1 in the last quarter of 1974; from 44.5 to 32.3, and from 42.5 to 26.8, in the first and second quarters of 1975, respectively). For 1975 even the lower exhaustion rates overstate the rate of exhaustion of all payments, for they include as exhaustees those who moved from Extended to Federal Supplemental Benefits and found work before their additional entitlement ran out. The likely success of Extended Benefits in preventing hardship before 1975 is illustrated by Hight using data from Pennsylvania and Georgia through 1974.[10] He demonstrates that even with insured unemployment at 7 percent (its peak for the country as a whole before 1975), a maximum potential duration of thirty-nine weeks would have been sufficient to push the total exhaustion rate to almost its lowest value in the postwar period.

The increased potential duration afforded by the extended programs produces economic effects similar to those of an increase in potential duration under regular programs. We saw that increased potential duration raises the average duration of unemployment, and it seems clear that the extension of benefits causes some slight increase in actual unemployment duration even of recipients of regular benefits. A regular UI claimant will be slightly more willing to resist accepting a lower-paying job if he knows that he can receive Extended Benefit payments if he exhausts his regular entitlement. The

43

only evidence on this point suggests that the existence of such payments in Nevada lengthened the duration of regular claims by three weeks.[11] This figure is probably very high, as is the estimate by Hanna et al. of the effect of increased potential duration of regular benefits, but it does illustrate empirically the possibility that Extended Benefits can affect the duration of regular claims. In any case, the effects on number and duration of spells of unemployment of those who would otherwise have taken jobs are the only real effects of an extended program. All others merely represent transfers of resources among individuals (from UI taxpayers to recipients of Extended Benefits) or measured changes in labor-force status, from out of the labor force to unemployed.

There is little doubt that extended programs induce some exhaustees of regular benefits to remain in the labor force rather than drop out. In all postwar recessions before that of 1973–75 the number of employed and unemployed individuals as a percentage of the adult population (labor-force participation rate) dropped. In the 1973–75 recession this number stayed essentially constant, even though industrial-output data suggest that the demand for labor during that time fell more (in percentage terms) than in previous postwar recessions. This phenomenon can be attributed to many other factors, including the possibility that the length and severity of the 1973–75 recession and the consequent desire to maintain earnings induced a net addition of workers to the labor force. However, the existence of substantial extensions of the potential duration of UI payments and the extension of coverage through Special Unemployment Assistance may be one cause. Although the recipients probably would not have been employed in the absence of inadequate labor demand, the presence of extended payment of UI benefits may have induced at least some of them to report themselves as unemployed rather than as out of the labor force in the monthly household survey, thus raising the civilian unemployment rate.

A claimant who exhausts his benefits can remain in the labor force as an unemployed job seeker, find employment when his UI benefits run out, or drop out of the labor force because job prospects appear slim, because he has returned to school, or because he has assumed responsibilities at home. Numerous studies of the labor-market experience of exhaustees in different states were conducted in the 1950s and 1960s.[12] They show that exhaustees who find new employment within six months after exhausting benefits (20–40 percent of all exhaustees) are most likely to do so within the first month. They also demonstrate that only a small fraction of exhaustees of regular state benefits in the recessions of 1958 and 1961 dropped out of the labor force after exhausting benefits. These results were corroborated in a study of exhaustees of regular and Extended Benefits in 1974–75.[13] Furthermore, the exhaustees in these studies showed a strong attachment to the labor force before they filed their initial claims. It appears that most claimants who eventually exhaust their benefits are not merely those who but for UI would have dropped out of the labor force.

The insured-unemployment rate is defined as the ratio of UI claimants to the number of covered employees. The number of claimants in turn depends upon the number and duration of spells of insured unemployment. Both increased average potential duration and easier eligibility for benefits (through lower required earnings and weeks of employment during the base period) raise the insured-unemployment rate by increasing the number of spells and/or duration of periods of insured unemployment. Consider the effect of increased potential duration of regular benefits. As noted in the comparison of New York and South Carolina, the uniform twenty-six-week potential duration leads to low exhaustion rates in New York, while South Carolina, with its variable and usually lower potential duration, usually has higher exhaustion rates. This difference may be caused by differences in actual labor-market conditions in the two states. It also may be causing systematic variation in measured insured-unemployment rates. For example, if South Carolina had had the same uniform potential duration and exhaustion rate of regular benefits as New York, we estimate that insured-unemployment rates in South Carolina would have been 5.0, 1.8, and 1.4 percent in 1961, 1969, and 1973, respectively, instead of 4.3, 1.6, and 1.3 percent. For the fourth quarter of 1974 the rate would have been 5.3 instead of 4.6 percent. Even more striking changes could be produced by comparing a state such as South Carolina with one such as Pennsylvania, which has an even longer uniform potential duration of benefits.

These calculations are not an academic exercise. Under many federal programs—for example, the Comprehensive Employment and Training Act of 1973 (CETA), economic development grants, and defense procurement—disbursements are based partly on state and area unemployment rates. These rates are constructed from data on insured unemployment, but our calculations demonstrate that the underlying data will vary depending on the provisions of state laws. While various techniques are used to try to account for these differences, they are a poor substitute for area data based on household surveys rather than the UI system, and they probably introduce inequity into the disbursement of funds under these programs. (They also cause considerable political controversy. Near the trough of the 1973–75 recession several governors claimed the calculated unemployment rates caused their states to lose public-service employment funds to which they were entitled under CETA.)[14] Furthermore, Extended Benefits, which can be triggered by the state's insured-unemployment rate rather than by any adjusted version, are more likely to go to states with high average potential duration of regular benefits (and thus a higher insured rate at each level of labor-market tightness).

The intention here is to indicate that exhaustion rates, duration of benefits, and insured-unemployment rates must be discussed with care. Some exhaustions will occur so long as there is a limit on potential duration of benefits. How many exhaustions should occur and what the exhaustion rate should be depend on one's views about the role of UI as a device for maintaining incomes. In discussing this issue, though, the analyst or policymaker should note that the relevant exhaustion rate for his purpose is based on exhaustions of all benefits. This rate will always be less than the widely reported exhaustion rate of regular benefits. The UI system does a better job of maintaining incomes of claimants during a recession than is indicated by commonly cited data.[15] Similarly, possible effects of differences in potential duration—both interstate and over time—on measured unemployment should be considered in any analysis or policy discussion that hinges upon a comparison of actual labor-market conditions.

Estimates of Supply Effects on the Civilian Unemployment Rate

The UI system affects the measured unemployment rate in a number of complex ways. Some have been outlined already, and they will form the basis for our calculations of the UI system's impact on unemployment. The effects on aggregate spending and thus the ability to smooth out cyclical fluctuations in output are discussed in chapter 4, as are the effects on the demand for labor induced by imperfect experience rating. The evidence in this section is based only on changes in duration and labor-force participation (supply behavior).

The policy importance of the system's effect on unemployment rates is obvious. A more immediate question is the effect of the temporary programs—Federal Supplemental Benefits and Special Unemployment Assistance—on both the measured unemployment rate and the real amount of productive labor employed. Was the severity of the 1973–75 recession, the deepest since the 1930s, overstated by a .7-percentage-point increase in measured unemployment induced by these changes in the UI system, as claimed by the U.S. Council of Economic Advisors?[16] The extent of this bias presents an empirical question that we will answer and that should be considered in structuring emergency programs in response to future recessions.

Although the many effects of the UI system on the unemployment rate suggest the necessity of constructing impact estimates piecemeal, some researchers have produced direct estimates of the total effect. This approach has serious problems. If we use data on different states, the impact of a more liberal UI system on unemployment is difficult to disentangle from the effects of perpetually higher unemployment on the political decision to increase the generosity of a state's system. This chicken-and-egg problem makes the comparison of interstate differences in unemployment rates a risky affair even in the absence of other difficulties. The use of historical data for the entire United States risks attributing changes in unemployment to changes in UI benefits when the true cause is some other, contemporaneous change in the structure of the economy.

A better approach is to construct estimates by examining the likely magnitudes of the various effects on unemployment created by workers' behavior. This method allows us to distinguish real changes in unemployment, resulting from shifts between employment and unemployment and producing losses in market output, from measured changes, produced by movements between unemployment and nonparticipation in the labor force; and it illustrates the mechanisms by which UI affects the behavior of labor.

For illustrative purposes, policy 1 will simulate the size of both real and measured changes in the unemployment rate induced by regular state benefits. We will also consider policy 2, an extension of coverage to 9 million additional workers, raising the fraction of covered employment by .10, from .75 to .85 of the labor force. Although the twenty-six weeks of Special Unemployment Assistance included when the legislation was first passed in December 1974 covered several million more people, it is likely that many were unaware of their eligibility. The 9-million figure is very close to that implied in permanent extensions of coverage proposed in 1975 and 1976. [17] As such, its estimated effect on unemployment should provide a guide to what will occur if UI coverage is broadened. All of these calculations are based on the assumption that nothing else changes, that the impact of the particular policy has been isolated, and that there is no effect on the number of spells of unemployment.

The effects of the policies are analyzed for different degrees of labor-market tightness. This analysis is essential. For example, evidence earlier in this chapter showed that during a recession higher potential duration is much more likely to induce individuals to remain in the labor force drawing benefits. While the determination of an appropriate unemployment rate to denote low unemployment is subject to debate, we arbitrarily assume it to be 4 percent. The recession total-unemployment rate is assumed to be 7.3 percent, corresponding roughly to a 10-percent shortfall of gross national product (GNP) from what it would be at low unemployment. The 7.3-percent rate is below that of the 1973–75 recession, above that of 1970–71, but near that reached in the 1958 and 1961 recessions. (It is not adjusted for changes in the demographic structure of the labor force that introduce changes in the total unemployment rate over time.) Each of these figures is a hypothetical rate assumed to prevail in the absence of policy 1. We then can gauge the role of UI in changing the unemployment rates observed at low and high levels of unemployment.

Effect 1 is the increased duration of unemployment among workers firmly attached to the labor force. It is a real increase that lowers employment and raises unemployment. We use the figure of .5 weeks extra actual duration in response to each 10-percentage-point increase in replacement when labor markets are tight, based on the studies summarized in table 4. With a gross replacement rate of 50 percent, the effect of regular benefits is an extra 2.5 weeks average duration (.5 times 5) if we extrapolate the .5-week effect. Since the impact on duration is much less when unemployment is high, we assume that a .1-week increase in duration is produced then by each extra 10 percentage points in the replacement rate, a total effect of .5 (.1 times 5). This figure is arbitrary, but it does reflect the sketchy evidence on differences in the effects of benefits on average duration over the business cycle.

The impact of effect 1 can be calculated using the average duration of insured unemployment in the low-unemployment year 1969, 11.6 weeks. Of this figure we can attribute 2.5 weeks to UI, so that we estimate UI benefits raise the average duration of spells of insured unemployment by 27 percent (2.5/9.1). In 1969 insured unemployment was 47 percent of civilian unemployment. At the hypothetical 4-percent total-unemployment rate, insured unemployment would be 1.88 percent (4.0 times .47). Thus policy 1 induces an extra .51 percentage points (.27 times 1.88) of unemployment through its effect on duration. At

49

high unemployment the assumed change in duration induced by regular benefit payments is .5 weeks, and the average duration of insured unemployment in the high-unemployment year 1961 was 14.7 weeks. The ratio (.5/14.2) is multiplied by .0365, the hypothetical fraction of insured unemployed in the total labor force at 7.3 percent civilian unemployment, based upon experience in 1961, to give a .13-percentage-point effect at high unemployment.

For policy 2, extending coverage to raise the fraction of the labor force covered by UI from .75 to .85, the effects can be estimated as .13 (.10 divided by .75) times the impact of policy 1. The .13 figure can be applied to all the estimated effects of policy 1 to derive the impact of policy 2. This simple procedure over-estimates the true impact, since newly covered workers probably experience lower unemployment than the average covered worker (see chapter 5).

Effect 2 is a measured effect only, reflecting those unemployed workers who otherwise would have left the labor force but who were induced to remain unemployed by the existence of higher UI benefits or longer potential duration. We assume this effect to be zero at low unemployment. At high unemployment we assume arbitrarily that twenty-six weeks of regular benefits induce the average worker to delay dropping out of the labor force for two weeks. (This may be an overestimate, given evidence on the strong labor-force attachment of exhaustees shown in Murray and Mathematica.)[18] Taking 14 percent (the ratio of this figure to 14.7, average duration during the 1961 recession) and multiplying by .0365, the hypothetical fraction of the labor force which would receive UI benefits at 7.3 percent civilian unemployment, gives a .51-percentage-point increase in the measured-unemployment rate produced by the provision of regular benefits. Since the labor-force participation of the majority of workers is quite insensitive to economic conditions, the assumption of two weeks extra average duration may be extreme. It implies that UI benefits induce an extra six weeks of measured unemployment per annum and an equal decrease in the time spent out of the labor force among the roughly one third of the labor force—youths 16–24 years of age and workers

55 + years—whose participation is probably somewhat sensitive to changes in labor-market conditions.

Effect 3 is also a measured effect only. It reflects how many persons who otherwise would not be seeking work are induced by the existence of UI benefits to enter the labor force. At an unemployment rate of 7.3 percent this effect is likely to be zero. When there are no jobs available, people will not suddenly enter the labor market and search for work because of the presence of UI benefits during their next spell of unemployment. On the other hand, at low unemployment the labor force will be swollen by people induced to enter partly by the knowledge that jobs are quickly available and that UI benefits can act as a cushion to their income after they have had some employment experience.

Instituting benefits is equivalent to an increase in expected earnings for workers considering entering the labor force. Their decision will reflect the response of their supply of labor to increases in the income expected (earnings and UI benefits) from work. We assume, following related evidence from Cain and Watts,[19] that labor-force participation rates for this group increase by .25 percent with each one-percent rise in expected incomes if no other changes occur. This figure is applied to the expected percentage increase in earnings plus benefits. If those workers induced to enter the labor force are unemployed six times as often as the average worker (24 percent of the time), the expected increase in earnings plus benefits is 6 percent (.24 times an average net replacement rate of .5 times the half of UI taxes not borne by labor). This implies a 1.50-percent (6 times .25) increase in the secondary labor force, or a .50-percent increase in the total labor force (1.50 times the roughly one third of the total labor force accounted for by secondary workers). The change in the civilian unemployment rate induced by policy 1 is .10 percentage points (.50 times 20 percent—the difference between 24 percent, the unemployment rate assumed for these extra workers, and the average unemployment rate of 4 percent).

Table 5 lists our best estimates of the real and measured effects. The measured effect consists of effect 2 at high unemployment only and of effect 3 at low unemployment only.

The likeliest impact of the entire system of benefits on the unemployment rate induced by changes in workers' behavior is .61 percentage points at low unemployment. If in the absence of UI benefits the unemployment rate were 4 percent, we would find the measured unemployment rate at 4.61 percent of the labor force, assuming recipients would not otherwise have received income transfers affecting their labor-market behavior. Most (.51 percentage points) of this increase is real, the result of extra time spent searching for work by persons who would otherwise have been employed. This part of the increase is a real loss of productive resources if the extra search time is unproductive. (As noted earlier, the evidence on its productivity is quite mixed.) The other part of the total effect (.10 percentage points) results from induced entry of individuals with unstable employment patterns who otherwise would not be in the labor force.

Table 5. Estimated Supply Effects of Selected UI Policies on the Unemployment Rate (in percentage points)

	Regular benefits		Extended coverage	
	(1) At low unemployment	(2) At high unemployment	(3) At low unemployment	(4) At high unemployment
Real	+.51	+.13	+.07	+.02
Measured	+.10	+.51	+.01	+.07
Total	+.61	+.64	+.08	+.09

Doubtless there are errors due to the lack of available studies on all the aspects of behavior that interact to produce the estimates. This is especially likely for effect 3, which is based on (liberal) guesses about the propensity of induced entrants into the labor force to experience unemployment after taking their initial job. Effect 1, however, is based on an interpretation of the studies presented in table 4, so that our estimated total effect of .61 percentage points is at least partly accurate.

Although the unemployment rate rises because of the induced real and measured effects of UI, the number of employed workers need not fall. Through effect 3, individuals with unstable employment experiences are induced to enter the labor force. While they are unemployed much more than other labor-force participants, thus raising the unemployment rate, they do find employment part of the time because UI induces them to work for a wage that makes them attractive to prospective employers. These periods of employment can offset the decreased employment (increased unemployment) produced by effect 1 among workers who are strongly attached to the labor force. If the group of induced entrants is employed on the average only 76 percent of the time, as we assumed, total employment rises by .38 percent (.76 times the .50 percent of the labor force that we estimated this group to be). Effect 1 is partly offset, so that the net fall in employment is only .13 percentage points (.51 minus .38). Thus, while UI benefit payments raise the unemployment rate at low unemployment, the number of people employed remains essentially unchanged.

Our estimate of the effect of the system of regular benefits on unemployment during a recession induced by changes in workers' behavior is .64 percentage points, but most of the effect is measured. Only .13 percentage points of this extra unemployment are attributable to workers who are induced to spend extra time looking for work. The remainder of the higher unemployment rate is a measurement effect produced by the inducements UI benefits provide workers to remain in the labor force.

A .09-percentage-point effect is produced at high unemployment by the extention of coverage under policy 2, up to twenty-six weeks of benefits for previously uncovered workers. If this estimate is correct, the thirty-nine-week program, in effect from July 1975 through March 1977, could not have increased the unemployment rate by much more than .13 percentage points (.09 times 39 divided by 26). Nearly all of the increase in the unemployment rate from this source is a measurement effect only. The total impact of a permanent extension of coverage of regular benefits at low unemployment would be a .08-percentage-point increase in the aggregate unemployment rate.

To determine the total effect of the emergency unemployment-compensation legislation of 1974–75 we also need to know the effect of the twenty-six weeks of Federal Supplemental Benefits. We estimate this effect as .22 percentage points (.64, the effect of twenty-six weeks of regular state UI benefits on the unemployment rate, times .35, the exhaustion rate of Extended Benefits observed for the United States at the trough of the 1973–75 recession). The sum of the effects of the two temporary programs is .35 percentage points (.22 plus .13), which is substantially smaller than the .7 cited by the U.S. Council of Economic Advisors.[20] We can conclude that the unemployment rate at the trough of the 1973–75 recession (the second quarter of 1975) would have been 8.6 instead of the 8.9 percent actually measured. Certainly this adjustment makes that recession appear slightly less severe. One should remember, however, that even 8.6 percent unemployment is substantially above the unemployment rate of any other recession since the 1930s. Even accounting for the larger fraction of the labor force composed of youths and others with high unemployment, the 1973–75 recession was slightly deeper than the 1958 or 1961 recessions, previously the deepest postwar recessions.

Our calculations suggest that the provision of UI benefits induces changes in workers' behavior that have both real and measured effects on the rate of unemployment in the United States. The effect on the duration of unemployment must be weighed against the improvements a policy of income maintenance through UI possibly affords society in the form of more efficient job-search behavior. In terms of the number of unemployed persons, the effects are important in two ways. First, most of the overall effect of the system has been with us since modern unemployment statistics began to be collected in the 1948 household survey. Its only policy significance is the implication that UI benefits provide an additional reason why the unemployment rate cannot be forced too low, that is, why "full employment" cannot be defined as an unemployment rate of zero. Second, and more important for policy purposes, the measured effect of extensions of benefits and coverage is small but not zero. This means that we must adjust indicators of unemployment when discussing the appropriate fiscal and monetary policies to move the economy out of a recession.

Specific Policy Issues

The major policy issues implicit in the discussion of the effect of UI on workers' behavior are clearly the amount and maximum potential duration of benefits. However, since these issues also affect employers' behavior and are linked closely to the question of eligibility, we will leave them for the concluding chapter. Based on the discussion of this chapter alone, only trigger mechanisms for extended programs, the incentive effects of partial-benefit payments, and the potential duration of regular benefits can be addressed.

The issue of *triggers for extended-benefit programs* is one that has pervaded much of the discussion of UI reform since the early 1960s. Assuming it is wise to have extended programs during recessions (an issue of maximum potential duration), should these be triggered automatically? and if so, how? The fundamental issue involves a political trade-off. Can the legislative process act quickly enough to obviate the need for an automatic mechanism that deprives elected representatives of their chance to react to events and attempt to alleviate people's immediate problems? The evidence of the 1974–75 amendments, which suggests that the reaction can be very rapid, implies that speed may not in practice be a great advantage for automatic triggers. Even if it is rapid, though, the lack of opportunity for careful construction of emergency programs would tip the balance in favor of an automatic trigger.

The current system of Extended Benefits uses both national and state insured-unemployment rates to trigger payments. As we have shown, the nature of state legal provisions on potential duration and eligibility guarantees that insured rates can differ greatly among states at the same degree of labor-market tightness. If Extended Benefits are to be based on conditions in area labor markets, it hardly makes sense to be paying in one area but not in another with the same conditions. Furthermore, the federal-state sharing of financing of Extended Benefits means that workers in those states with stringent eligibility requirements and short average potential duration among exhaustees of regular benefits, where Extended Benefits are unlikely to be paid (because insured-unemployment rates are low), will bear part of the cost of extended programs in other states. Both arguments suggest one of two options: Either only the national insured rate should be used as a triggering mechanism or area or state total-unemployment rates, which are adjusted to reflect interstate differences in UI laws, should be used. Also, if the state insured rate is maintained as a triggering device, the necessity for ad hoc waiving of the requirement that the current rate be 120 percent of the previous two years' should be permanently removed. It makes no sense to maintain in the law a provision that must be amended repeatedly, nor should a state with high but constant unemployment be barred from paying extended benefits.

A second policy concerns *partial benefits*. A worker can earn some fraction of weekly benefit payments during partial unemployment without jeopardizing his receipt of benefits, and some dollar amount of earnings is often disregarded before benefits start being reduced. Partial-benefit schedules often contain large potential disincentives. For example, in Michigan, Nebraska, and Wisconsin the full weekly benefit is paid so long as the claimant's earnings are below half the weekly amount. Should his earnings rise above that, he receives only half the full benefit; when his earnings equal the full benefit, he receives nothing. This means that a worker with a full benefit of $40 can earn $19.99 and enjoy a total income of $59.99, but if he earns $20.01, his income will be only $40.01. Similarly, he can earn $39.99 and have an income of $59.99 or earn $40.01 and have an income of $40.01. An extra two pennies earned result in an income loss of $19.98. These are extreme cases, but most other states have partial-benefit schedules with implied disincentives nearly as peculiar.

Munts shows, not very surprisingly, that a disproportionate fraction of workers on partial benefits in Wisconsin earn either slightly less than half the full weekly benefit or slightly less than the full benefit. [21] Partial benefits are explicitly designed to supplement the income of workers on short hours and to encourage those who are totally unemployed to take part-time work. That the partial-benefit schedules apparently discourage work to some extent seems to contradict in part the purpose of this aspect of the UI program. This issue is not a major problem of the system; for example, recipients of partial benefits constituted only 5 percent of all recipients in the first quarter of 1975 (and they received a much lower percentage of all payments). Nonetheless, other states could adopt, and a federal law containing benefit standards should encourage, the provision of partial-benefit schedules such as those in Connecticut, Kentucky, Nevada, and Washington, where benefit payments are reduced by less than one dollar with each additional dollar of part-time earnings. (The reduction rates are $.67, $.80, $.75, and $.75, respectively.) With more widespread adoption of schedules like these, partial benefits could better achieve the goal of maintaining incomes while providing an incentive to seek full-time work.

The question of *variable versus uniform potential duration* has been answered differently in different states. The economic issue is whether variable potential duration up to twenty-six weeks, linked to the claimant's prior work experience in covered employment, produces less time unemployed or in wasteful job search than would uniform potential duration of twenty-six weeks. The answer depends on the effect of increased potential duration of benefits on unemployment among those workers in variable-duration states who currently do not qualify for the maximum potential duration. The few studies cited in this chapter indicate that increased potential duration of regular benefits produces some increase in the average duration of unemployment. However, the bulk of this increase occurs when labor markets are loose, which suggests that it is largely a measured effect rather than a real loss in employed resources. We also saw that exhaustees in variable-duration states whose potential duration is less than the maximum are disproportionately workers who may be less closely attached to the labor force. This suggests that for them, even more than for other beneficiaries, the real effect of increased potential duration is quite small. Despite these considerations, some (probably small) real loss is induced by allowing all beneficiaries a twenty-six-week potential duration. This factor, coupled with the transfer of resources to claimants whose attachment to the labor force is likely to be weak, suggests that potential duration should be variable up to the maximum. Workers with more quarters of prior covered earnings should receive benefits for a longer time than those whose experience makes them barely eligible for benefits.

4

The UI System and the Employer

Just as unemployment-insurance benefits and taxes affect the behavior of workers in diverse ways, they also produce changes in employers' demand for labor. In the broad context of the national economy, the provision of benefits to unemployed workers who are also consumers can serve to maintain product demand during recessions and prevent employment from falling precipitously. Benefits and experience-rated taxes that affect workers' willingness to work in different firms interact to change the pattern of layoffs over the year and over the business cycle and may also affect the mix of output produced. Finally, the ceiling on the tax base may affect the mix of skilled and unskilled workers that the employer uses in his production process. The first two of these three demand effects operate through variations in employment and unemployment. The third produces a continuing constant difference in the numbers of skilled and unskilled workers employed. We estimate the size of the change in employment and/or unemployment produced by the first two effects only; existing data and knowledge do not permit estimation of the third.

How Does Unemployment Insurance Affect the Business Cycle?

Unemployment insurance is one of many automatic stabilizers built into the modern U.S. economy to slow declines in aggregate income. These include the personal income tax, corporate income taxes, and benefits and payroll taxes for Social Security. All of these automatically increase the size of the federal deficit during recessions by either increasing government expenditures or decreasing revenue. With a larger federal deficit during a recession, aggregate spending is maintained above what it otherwise would be, and this extra spending produces a greater than one-for-one effect on GNP because of induced increases in personal consumption. During a cyclical recovery the opposite effect occurs: Expenditures decline and revenues accruing through these automatic devices rise. At that time an automatic stabilizer can inhibit the economy from reaching a condition of excess aggregate demand and prevent it from overheating and generating an inflation induced by shortages in product and labor markets.

Automatic stabilizers, including UI, are instruments of fiscal policy. As such, their effectiveness in stimulating GNP and thus employment demand depends on the overall efficacy of fiscal-policy tools. A great debate on this issue has raged among economists over the last twenty years, and there has been no resolution, either by overwhelming evidence or by devastating theoretical argument. One side argues that no fiscal measure, automatic or otherwise, can be effective without a corresponding change in the supply of money. The other side argues that stimulatory fiscal policy can affect output, even in the absence of changes in the supply of money, by encouraging businesses and consumers to use their existing holdings of money more rapidly.

This important debate cannot be resolved here, but we must make some tentative conclusion in order to be able to draw inferences about the effect of UI alone on GNP. For purposes of discussion we will take the position implied in the second view, namely, that UI benefits and taxes produce changes in GNP even in the absence of changes in the supply of money. This view is implicit in the studies summarized later. However, one must recognize the possible validity of the argument that stabilization works only because the Federal Reserve finances the deficits resulting from UI benefits by increasing the supply of money. If this is true, there is nothing automatic about the stabilization, for its apparent effect depends upon the discretionary actions of the Federal Reserve allowing the benefits to affect demand, not upon the benefits themselves.

It is also possible that in the absence of UI, individuals would save more during good times to maintain their consumption when they experience unemployment. To the extent that this would occur, UI would displace some private saving during booms and some private spending during a recession. There is no evidence on the extent of this displacement, but by failing to include this effect in our calculations we are probably over-estimating the cushion provided to aggregate spending in a recession by the disbursement of UI benefits.

The payment of UI benefits acts as an automatic stabilizer in two ways. Most important and obvious, as the economy slides into a recession, more covered workers begin receiving benefits as they become unemployed. A second spur to the payment of benefits is produced by the changing skill mix that occurs among unemployed beneficiaries as the recession deepens. Because UI benefits are linked to prior earnings, the increasing fraction of unemployed who are skilled workers causes benefits per worker to rise during a recession. For both reasons—increased numbers of beneficiaries and increased payments per beneficiary—benefit payments increase. A striking example of this occurred between the first quarters of 1974 and 1975, when payments of regular benefits increased from $1.7 billion to $3.6 billion.

At first glance UI taxes appear to be an automatic destabilizer that could rise in recessions and fall in expansions. Since the tax is experience rated, firms must increase their tax payments to replace reserves depleted during a recession. The individual firm moves to a higher tax rate on its state's schedule, and the state as a whole moves to a higher schedule as its pooled funds become depleted. This process does indeed take place, but it occurs slowly relative to the duration of the business cycle. In all states there are lags before a higher or lower rate schedule is applied to employers. Furthermore, most reserve-ratio states base the ratio on a three-year average of payrolls, and other experience-rating systems are usually based on three years of benefit experience. Even if funds suddenly become depleted by a sharp recession, the gap is not immediately filled by increases in taxes. Since postwar business cycles generally have lasted three to five years, UI taxes can have a neutral or even stabilizing effect on aggregate demand. Furthermore, because tax collections decline over the calendar year due to the limit on the tax base, depending on the timing of a recession, they could produce countercyclical fluctuations in the government surplus. The extent of stabilization (or destabilization) produced by both benefit payments and employer taxes is really an empirical issue.

Six studies have attempted to gauge the effectiveness of UI in preventing deep recessions in the United States. The evidence from this research is summarized in table 6. None of the studies implies that UI has prevented more than one fourth of the cyclical decline in GNP that would otherwise have occurred. Given the incomplete coverage of employment, the ineligibility of many unemployed persons, the lack of compensation for lost overtime, and the loss of nonlabor income that also occurs during recessions, this failure is hardly surprising. Four studies calculate the effectiveness of UI in three or more recessions.[1] Their quite similar results imply that postwar recessions would have been roughly 10 to 20 percent more severe in the absence of the UI program. The lower of these figures is the best estimate of the effect, for one cannot, as is done in most studies, attribute all changes in GNP to changes in fiscal policy.

All the studies in table 6 base their calculations on the variation in benefit payments over cycle, but only three include variations in taxes, and only Clement and Rejda estimate the countercyclical effect of UI taxes separately.[2] The results suggest that the destabilizing effect of tax collections either does not exist or is dwarfed by the stabilizing effect of benefit payments. This conclusion is strengthened by comparing Eilbott's results, using benefits minus taxes, with those of the other studies. His estimated effect is small, but it is still greater than zero.

Table 6. Studies of the Countercyclical Effects of UI Benefits and Taxes

Study	Time period (recession)	Percent change in spending accounted for by UI
Clement (1960)	Average peak to trough, 1949 and 1954;	
	benefits	+26.2
	taxes	− 1.7
Duesenberry et al. (1960)	1958; benefits	+10.8
Eilbott (1966)	Average peak to trough, 1949, 1954, and 1958; benefits minus taxes	+ 9.0
Lewis (1962)	Average peak to trough, 1949, 1954, 1958, and 1961; benefits	+11.9
Rejda (1966)	Average peak to trough, 1949, 1954, 1958, and 1961;	
	benefits	+24.0
	taxes	0
von Furstenberg (1976)	Average of 1958, 1961, and 1971; benefits	+16.5

None of the studies includes estimates for the 1973–75 recession, but it is likely that the UI system as a whole had a greater effect in it than in earlier postwar recessions. The introduction of Federal Supplemental Benefits and Special Unemployment Assistance added to the federal deficit and thus to the stimulatory effect on aggregate demand. However, these new programs were not part of the automatic effect of UI but were instead discretionary fiscal measures that may not be reintroduced in future recessions. Thus they are more appropriately classified with other discretionary fiscal policies (increased highway construction, military spending, and so forth). The stabilizing effect of *automatic* changes in UI benefit payments in the 1973–75 recession was probably close to what it was in previous recessions.

Eilbott has shown that automatic stabilizers are much more successful in preventing deep recessions than they are in preventing the excess aggregate demand that occurs near the end of cyclical expansions.[3] Indeed, Clement shows that UI in particular has virtually no effect as a stabilizer during expansions but a substantial effect in preventing further declines in output during recessions.[4] This evidence suggests that as an aggregate measure UI benefits and taxes function quickly and effectively to prevent even greater drops in employment (rises in unemployment) during recessions and that they have small, slow restraining effects on employment increases during expansions. They lower the variability of unemployment over the cycle by keeping it from falling as far as it would in their absence. In chapter 3 we assumed that the civilian unemployment rate rose an average of 3.3 percentage points from the peak of the business cycle to the trough. (This approximates the average rise of 3.0 percentage points in recessions between 1957 and 1975.) If UI as an automatic stabilizer prevents a 10-percent decline in real GNP, we can infer that the unemployment rate would rise by an extra .33 percentage points (.10 times 3.3) without UI.

Although UI has cushioned only 10 percent of the cyclical declines in GNP that have occurred since 1948, it appears to have been the greatest single automatic stabilizing force during the first two postwar recessions.[5] This is a very strong argument in favor of maintaining some automatic form of payments to eligible unemployed workers, since it is unlikely that discretionary fiscal policy can always operate so quickly. As long as we think fiscal policy has an effect on fluctuations in demand, UI benefits are essential in preventing even wider swings in unemployment than now occur. Whether benefit-payment formulas should retain their current eligibility and duration requirements is irrelevant for this issue. The evidence is that unemployment benefits in some form must be paid automatically if we are to avoid substantially greater hardships during recessions of the kind that have prevailed since the 1940s.

Experience Rating and Employment: Subsidies and Wedges

Because of partial experience rating, an industry with a high unemployment experience will exhibit a higher tax rate than other industries. Indeed, as indicated in chapter 2, most of the variation in UI tax rates is across industries. Despite the higher tax rates paid by firms (and eventually by workers and consumers) in any industry characterized by high unemployment, we generally find that such an industry does not cover the costs of benefits paid to its former employees. In a fairly broad sample of states analyzed by Becker, over an eleven-year period benefit payments were roughly double UI tax payments in the same industries, agriculture and construction in particular.[6] In contrast, employees in finance, wholesale and retail trade, and public utilities received UI benefits that were one half to two thirds of the taxes paid in these industries. In effect, certain industries pay taxes that partly finance UI benefits paid in other industries. Construction, agriculture, and certain seasonal manufacturing industries are subsidized by other sectors of the economy. This results from maximum and nonzero minimum rates in experience-rating schedules.

How does this cross-subsidy affect the labor market? Let us assume the economy can be divided into two sectors. Workers in sector A know they will be unemployed for a relatively large but variable fraction of each year (possibly because product demand and production are very seasonal in nature). Workers in sector B expect to be unemployed only a small, variable fraction of each year. Before the advent of UI benefit payments and taxes the same worker might require $4 per hour to work in A but only $3 per hour to work in B. Labor costs in A are then significantly higher than in B because employers in A must compensate workers for the much higher risk of being unemployed. Because costs are higher in A, the prices of products sold in A will be higher if other things are equal.

Under UI an imperfect experience-rated system is introduced in which benefits in sector A are financed half by taxes paid in A and half by taxes paid in B. The lower total benefits in sector B are financed entirely by taxes in B. Although identical workers becoming unemployed in A or B receive the same benefit, the existence of benefits means much more in A. More workers become unemployed in A, and all workers welcome the cushion that benefits would provide should they become unemployed. Wages in sector A fall substantially in comparison with those in sector B because workers in A know their incomes will be maintained by UI benefits while they are unemployed. Part of the decrease in labor costs in sector A is wiped out by UI taxes paid there, but not all, for these taxes are less than the total of UI benefits paid to workers in A. In sector B, though, all benefits are supported through payroll taxes in this sector, and part of the benefits paid in A are also financed out of taxes paid in B. Not only is the small decline in operating costs through lower wages wiped out, but operating costs probably rise on net because taxes exceed benefits paid in B.

Because operating costs fall in sector A and rise in sector B, firms in A will make greater profits, while those in B will make less. After all adjustments take place prices will be lower in A and higher in B, while output will be higher in A and lower in B. As does any subsidy, the hidden UI subsidy leads to distortions in price, output, and employment patterns. Output is greater in seasonal industries, such as construction and agriculture, where benefits fall short of tax collections, and less elsewhere. Because output is shifted among sectors, employment is also shifted in the same directions. No unemployment is produced, but society is not using its resources as efficiently as possible because product prices do not reflect all costs of production. Prices are too low in sector A and too high in sector B. Although not intended to do so, if experience rating is not perfect, UI can provide incentives that lead to overproduction of products whose manufacture is characterized by high unemployment.

It is impossible to measure the overall effect of cross-subsidies through the UI system, but we can gauge the likely magnitude of the subsidy provided to a typical industry that does not finance all the benefits paid to its workers. In construction, for example, taxes were roughly 2.5 percent of taxable wages in covered employment between 1957 and 1967, while benefits approximated 5 percent in the states analyzed by Becker. [7] Benefits minus taxes were roughly 2.5 percent of taxable pay-rolls. The average ratio of taxable to total payrolls in all industries over this period was .59, but because construction is a high-wage industry, the ratio there was probably closer to .5. This implies that benefits minus taxes were 1.25 percent of total payrolls (2.5 times .5). Using 1.25 percent as an estimate and bearing in mind that construction labor comprises slightly over one third of construction costs, we estimate that the UI subsidy lowers the relative price of construction by .44 percent (.35, labor costs as a fraction of the value of new public and private construction in 1972, times 1.25). The demand for new construction is greater as a result of this price reduction by an amount that depends upon people's preferences for construction (new homes, factories, offices) vis-à-vis other items on which they spend.

One may argue that a subsidy of one-half percent of the price of new construction is small and that construction is an extreme example. (In most industries benefits and taxes diverge less.) On the other hand, we should remember that UI costs are a small part of total costs; benefits and taxes average only one percent of total wages in covered employment. By this comparison the labor cost and eventual price subsidy of construction (and a few other industries) appear much more substantial. The subsidy has clear detrimental economic effects and no obvious economic justification.

Because the UI tax is not perfectly experience rated, many layoffs result in no increase, present or future, in an employer's tax rate. Even if he is charged for the layoff and is not at the minimum or maximum tax rate, experience-rating plans are constructed so that it is several years before his tax rises to reflect fully the cost of a particular layoff. These factors—imperfect experience rating and future charging for current benefits—interpose a wedge between the private costs of a layoff and what the claimant receives. The cost to the rest of society (transfer of income from UI accounts to the eligible claimants) equals the claimant's benefits. The private cost, paid by the employer and probably shifted almost entirely backward to his employees or forward to his customers, is less than the benefit payment to the claimant. Neither of these costs reflects wasted resources, but they do affect behavior if they diverge.

What are the effects of this wedge on the behavior of employers and workers when demand for a firm's output drops? Let us assume that the employer expects demand for his product to be lower by some known amount and that he cannot just produce for inventory at the same rate of production as he maintains when product demand is higher. This is a very good characterization of a seasonal industry, in which regular variations in output are expected, but it is less satisfactory in describing cyclical changes in employment, since these are generally unexpected. Accordingly, this discussion applies best to the effects of the UI benefit-tax system on seasonal layoffs and thus on the unemployment rate at full employment. (A substantial fraction of UI benefits does accrue to those who are unemployed because of seasonal variations in output. Warden shows that about one third of payments in Massachusetts during the high-unemployment years 1958–62 were for seasonal unemployment.)[8]

Consider first a case in which there is no experience rating. Because workers know they will be compensated by UI benefits during their layoff (if they have sufficient base-period weeks of work and/or earnings), they are more willing than otherwise to work for an employer who frequently lays off workers. As do the next two cases, this argument depends on the layoffs being expected, so that workers and employers adjust their behavior completely to the prospect of changes in demand. When making a layoff decision, the employer knows the worker will be receiving benefits when laid off and will be satisfied with a lower rate of pay at the firm in the future because of those benefits. He also knows that those additional benefits cost him nothing because for him the system is not effectively experience rated. The wedge between the amount paid and the employer's costs of the layoff exactly equals the benefits the worker will receive. Compared with a case in which no UI benefits exist, the employer will be more likely to make the layoff. It does not cost the employer higher UI taxes, and because the worker will receive UI benefits, he works for lower wages, and the employer's production costs are lower. Some empirical evidence supporting this observation is provided by O'Connor, who shows that wages in moderately seasonal industries rose significantly less rapidly between 1939 and 1941, just after UI benefit payments were initiated, than in nonseasonal or very seasonal industries. [9]

(Workers in the most seasonal industries presumably were generally ineligible for the newly instituted UI benefits.) These differences were not observed over any other two-year period between 1933 and 1947.

Since in most states partial experience rating exists, the first case is not widely applicable. If the employer is taxed on the variable part of the schedule, he knows that the layoff will raise his UI tax bill in the future. In this second case the wedge is smaller. The employer will be much less willing to lay the worker off, for he will bear the cost of the benefits in the form of higher future UI taxes. (If he shifts the additional taxes backward to his employees, they will be less willing to work for him, and his operating costs will rise. If he shifts them forward, he will lose customers.) No matter who actually bears the tax initially, the employer has more of an incentive to retain the worker in the second case than in the first. He is, however, more likely to make the layoff than if there were no UI system. Even though he, his employees, or his customers must bear the higher tax, it will be in the future, while the benefits to the worker (and to the firm, since the worker is more willing to work in a seasonal industry) accrue immediately. Furthermore, since the benefits currently are not taxed, even complete and immediate experience rating would still produce more layoffs than if there were no UI. Since workers benefit more from a dollar of UI benefits than from a dollar of wages, the firm's labor costs fall as wages adjust down when benefits are higher. This in turn induces more layoffs than otherwise.

The third case, in which the employer is already at the maximum rate on the state's highest schedule or at a nonzero minimum rate on its lowest schedule, is exactly analogous to the first. The wedge between the costs to the state's UI account and to the employer of making the layoff again equals the benefits the worker will be paid. The employer has much less incentive to retain the worker than he had in the second case, in which he was on the variable part of the tax schedule.

In the third case, as in the first, the tax structure of the UI system encourages the growth of a labor force with a weak attachment to work and consequently little incentive to acquire skills. The effect on seasonal variation in employment is undoubtedly significant. Even more important, although much more difficult to quantify, may be the loss to society because some members of the labor force are discouraged from acquiring skills that they would have attained in the absence of UI, or in the presence of a perfectly experience-rated UI system. This loss contributes to the creation of a secondary work force that is difficult to integrate into the mainstream of the economy.

The net effect of UI is almost certainly to increase the amount of seasonal variation in employment and unemployment over what it would be if there were no system. The extent of this increase is reduced by effective experience rating, but even in a system that is completely, but not immediately, experience rated, employment variation will be more than it would in the absence of UI.

Depending upon the employer's position on his state's tax schedules, the wedge can vary from almost zero, if experience rating is effective, to the entire amount of benefits that the potential layoff would receive, if it is not effective. Using data from Becker, we find that for the United States as a whole in 1967, 19 percent of a weighted average of taxable payrolls was at an effective minimum rate, while 9.2 percent was at the maximum.[10] It is impossible to tell whether 1967 is typical. At the very least, though, we can conclude that experience rating was not effective within this one year for employers representing perhaps as much as one third of taxable payrolls. Since Becker also shows that in 1967 benefits charged to firms with negative balances in their accounts ranged from 25 to 62 percent of all benefits in the eight states examined, the one-third figure appears reasonable by this measure too.[11] The figure may contain errors for several possibly offsetting reasons. Insofar as current benefits are only reflected in taxes paid in the future, it understates the effect. It also ignores spells of unemployment induced among workers who quit in order to receive UI benefits after a long waiting period (in states where they are not disqualified for the duration of a spell of unemployment). On the other hand, the calculation is based on the tax schedules applicable in 1967. It ignores the existence of multiple tax schedules and thus overstates the fraction of taxable payrolls that is at the minimum or maximum tax rate in the entire set of schedules.

In the absence of the UI system an employer considering laying off a worker will save simply the total compensation—the wages and fringe benefits not paid. Since weekly benefits are roughly 50 percent of weekly wages, the wedge is one sixth of weekly wages (.50 times one third). Wage payments in 1974 were roughly 93 percent of total compensation, so the wedge was 16 percent of the savings an employer would make if he laid off a worker (one sixth of .93). The lowered cost of a layoff induces more layoffs. If the firm responds proportionately, the wedge accounts for 16 percent of seasonal layoffs in covered employment.

We can apply the 16-percent figure directly to the layoff rate. The effect on spells of unemployment can then be used to derive the effect on the unemployment rate, since we are assuming here that duration and the labor force are constant. In manufacturing, the only sector for which data are available, between 1958 and 1969 seasonal variation in layoffs was 31 percent of the total variation in layoffs. (This figure is quite consistent with Warden's evidence for Massachusetts.) [12] Seasonal variation in layoffs thus accounts for roughly .62 percentage points of an unemployment rate of 4 percent (.31 times 4.0 times the 50 percent of spells of unemployment accounted for on the average by layoffs). If 16 percent of this is due to the UI wedge and three fourths of the labor force is covered by UI, the unemployment rate is higher by .075 percentage points than it would be if the system were perfectly experience rated (.62 times .16 times .75). In other words, our best estimate is that the imperfect experience-rated system of unemployment insurance accounts for 1.9 percent (.075/4.00) of unemployment spells at low unemployment.

Because workers and employers expect seasonal variations in output, they have time to adjust their behavior and use the UI system to cushion the effects of these variations. This is less likely to occur during cyclical declines in output, for these come at unpredictable intervals. Nonetheless, some of the arguments we have used for seasonal layoffs apply also, albeit with less force, to cyclical layoffs. There is no empirical evidence available on this effect, nor is the simple arithmetic we have used to measure the seasonal effect applicable to unexpected (cyclical) output changes. However, the small size of the seasonal effect makes the likely cyclical effect fairly small.

There is weak evidence from employer surveys that experience rating has some slight stabilizing effect. In two separate surveys cited by Becker, 25 and 15 percent, respectively, of the employers interviewed attribute their efforts to stabilize employment to the experience-rated tax.[13] Survey evidence about what people *think* they have done is a poor substitute for careful measurement of what they *actually* have done; but these data provide some support for the conclusion that compared with a UI system financed by a uniform tax, experience rating has some (probably small) effect on employment variations.

The Tax Base and Its Effects

Unlike the tax base for Social Security, which has been raised since the early 1960s to cover most of the payroll, the tax base for UI has been eroded relative to payrolls. In 1940 the $3,000 base enabled the program to subsume 93 percent of total payrolls. By 1971 this figure had fallen to 45 percent, and even the increase in the tax base to $4,200 effective in 1972 was not sufficient to keep taxable payrolls from dropping to 48 percent of total payrolls in 1974. Without further federal legislation this figure will fall even further. Even with labor turnover, which, as we saw in chapter 1, increases the size of taxable payrolls, the taxable payroll per covered employee was only $4,367 in 1974. This evidence suggests that state laws providing for a tax base above $4,200 and the presence of labor turnover are relatively ineffective in increasing the amount of wages subject to the UI tax.

In the long run the effects of a higher tax base are not clear. State experience-rating schedules may be changed by legislation to reflect the higher base and to prevent an excess accumulation of reserves. Similarly, some states that might have raised the tax base on their own will refrain from doing so.

Nonetheless, the evidence that it was the federal increase effective in 1972 which temporarily reversed the erosion relative to total payrolls suggests that an increase in the base would substantially increase collections for a number of years. It would also affect the degree of effective experience rating, employers' choices about how to respond to changes in product demand, and the choice whether to employ low- or high-wage workers.

The net impact of a higher tax base on the degree of experience rating is unclear, but some effects seem likely. First, high-wage employers now at their state's highest tax rate (in construction, for example) would pay higher taxes on most of their employees. They would be hardest hit by any increase. Second, low-wage employers at their state's highest rate would experience higher taxes on those employees now earning more than the tax base. Since most workers in a low-wage firm earn at most only slightly more than the tax base, the firm's UI tax payments would not be increased greatly. Third, unless the minimum rate on the lowest schedule were zero, high-wage employers at the minimum tax rate would experience a substantial increase in tax payments. Fourth, so long as they were not pushed to the minimum rate on the lowest schedule, the tax bills of high- and low-wage employers not currently at the minimum would not be affected for long by increases in the tax base. (If their experience did not change, their tax rates would be adjusted downward to prevent their reserve accounts from increasing.) In summary, while high-wage employers at the maximum rate before the base increase would pay taxes that more closely reflected their experience, high-wage employers currently near the minimum tax rate would be pushed down to that rate. The fraction of total payrolls at either the minimum or maximum tax rates could increase or decrease. Only in states where the minimum rate is zero would this fraction generally decrease and the number of employers whose UI taxes are affected by an additional charged benefit thus rise.

The limit on the tax base affects an employer's choice about how to meet increases in the demand for his product. In a firm where all employees earn at least $4,200 and none quits or is laid off, the employer incurs no additional UI tax charges if he expands weekly hours. If he hires another worker, however, he is charged an amount equal to $4,200 times his tax rate. This fact encourages the employer to expand employment during a recovery period more slowly than he otherwise would. The incentive could work the opposite way when demand for the employer's product declines during a recession. If he cuts hours, his tax bill may not change, and he surely incurs no new charged benefits. If he lays off employees, his tax bill may be reduced temporarily, and it will be reduced permanently if he is at the extremes of the state's tax schedules. For firms not at the extremes the likely incentive is to cut hours, but for firms at the extremes the incentive clearly is to lay off workers. Imperfect experience rating, coupled with the limit on the tax base, has a tendency to produce an asymmetric response to changes in demand, causing some firms to be less hesitant about laying off workers during a recession than about hiring new workers during an expansion. These considerations imply that increases in the tax base to some extent smooth fluctuations in employment, especially where quit rates are low, wages are high, and thus much of the payroll is not subject to tax.

Perhaps the most important effect of the low tax base is on the distribution of employment between high- and low-wage workers. We concluded in chapter 2 that the net distributional impact of the UI system is small. Because of the limitation of the tax base to $4,200 in 1975 and benefit maxima that become effective at base-period earnings above $4,200 in most states, an especially large share of the tax is eventually paid by low-wage workers. The net effect of the system on the relative employment of low- and high-wage workers depends on a comparison of the distribution of benefits with the distribution of that part of the tax burden borne by labor. Since benefits appear to be fairly evenly distributed by income class, while this part of the tax burden is borne heavily by low-wage workers, the net effect is a relative rise in the sum of earnings and UI benefits for high-wage workers as compared with low-wage workers. The net subsidy to enter the labor force is greater among highly skilled individuals, although it is likely that for both groups the system creates an incentive to work in the market rather than at home. (This was the cause of effect 3 in chapter 3.) Differences in the net subsidy according to skill level are greater to the extent that labor's share of the burden exceeds the half we estimated in chapter 2.

If the base were increased and nothing else were changed, employers would initially bear the increased taxes. Since the increase only affects the cost of employing workers earning above \$4,200, the greatest initial effect would be to raise the relative demand for low-wage workers. (The cost of employing them would drop relatively.) An increased tax base clearly would help improve the unemployment situation facing low-wage workers, at least initially; after a few years, though, half the extra taxes would be shifted backward onto workers. Since these extra taxes affect mainly higher-wage workers, these workers would bear a greater proportion of that half of the total burden that is borne by labor. Accordingly, the net subsidy to seek work would become relatively more favorable to low-wage workers. Their labor-force participation would rise relative to that of high-wage workers, especially since it is likely that the supply of low-wage workers is more responsive to increased rewards from work. Employment of low-wage individuals would then increase compared with that of other workers. Even if labor eventually paid the entire tax, so long as benefit maxima were not increased along with the increased base, work would become relatively more advantageous for low-wage people, and their relative supply would rise. The eventual effect of a higher tax base is in the same direction as the initial effect, but it works through changes in individuals' labor supply rather than through changes in employers' demands for the services of different groups of workers.

Specific Policy Issues

Our discussions demonstrate that improving the *extent of experience rating* would remove some of the cross-subsidies now produced by the UI system and would also lower slightly the number of seasonal layoffs. It would do this by eventually forcing consumers and workers attached to goods production that uses techniques that generate substantial unemployment to bear the cost of UI benefits paid to the unemployed and by removing the wedge between the layoff costs to the employer and to society. The more perfect the experience-rating scheme, the more desirable it becomes on economic grounds. An ideal system would have a zero minimum tax rate on its lowest tax schedules and a very high (or perhaps no) maximum tax rate on its highest schedule. Admittedly, current limitations on minimum and maximum tax rates are the result of political compromises over a forty-year period, and it is unreasonable to expect movement toward more perfect experience rating to be rapid. However, since experience-rating plans were given preference in the Social Security Act of 1935, which established the federal-state UI arrangement, there is no reason why the act could not be amended to define experience rating more specifically and thus induce states to change their plans in order to qualify for federal credit. Noncharged benefits could be financed by either state or federal flat-rate taxes on employees (see chapter 2) or by an increase in the .5-percent federal tax. The financing of these benefits need not interfere with the improvement of experience rating.

While perfect experience rating seems desirable at first glance, it conflicts in part with the automatic-stabilization features of UI. If we tried to remove that part of the wedge in layoff costs that results from tax increases lagging behind benefit charges, we would find the stabilizing effects of the combined benefits and taxes diminished. (Benefits rise as unemployment rises, while, as we have shown, taxes do not vary simultaneously with unemployment. Removing the wedge would make taxes also rise when unemployment rises, thus lessening the automatic stimulus to the economy during a recession.) The timing of tax increases should be left as is, in full recognition that part of the incentive for layoffs will remain in the system. So long as an employer's charged benefits are covered by taxes over a period of years (three to five), most of the current cross-subsidy and part of the incentive for layoffs would be removed. The entire effect could be removed if future taxes contained an interest penalty applied to past benefit charges. However, the complexity of the charging procedures required suggests that for political reasons, the simple delay of taxes, with no interest charge, is the best apparent compromise between the goals of lessening inefficiencies and inequities and retaining the beneficial effects in smoothing business cycles.

Despite the lag of tax increases behind charged benefits, after several years the increased benefits paid out during a recession become reflected in higher employer taxes. In most postwar recessions the cycle has been sufficiently short that the tax increases have come after the economic recovery was well under way. The length and depth of the 1973–75 recession produced a new experience: Taxes started to rise even while the economy was barely beginning to recover from the cyclical trough. The effects of this unusual situation on the path of an economic recovery are serious, and they have caused some concern among policymakers. [14] To avoid the inhibiting effect of tax increases during the early stages of a recovery, the intake into the UI loan funds through the federal tax must be increased through either an increase in the federal tax rate or an increase in the tax base. It is clear that if possible, the increase should be timed to become effective when the economy is at something resembling full employment.

Increasing the tax base has been put forth as a solution to the short-run fiscal difficulties of the UI system. For example, an increase to $8,000, coupled with a temporary rise in the federal tax to .7 percent, was reported by the House Ways and Means Committee in December 1975. Staff calculations suggested that this would increase states' collections by $4.5 billion over the $10 billion expected for 1977, when the higher base would become effective. [15] No doubt it would have this effect, but even more important is the eventual change it would bring in the economic effects of UI. Although the net impact of the system on the income distribution is small, the program provides incentives for all individuals to seek work outside the home, especially higher-wage workers. It does this because of the limitation on the tax base. If the base were raised, the system would probably favor those families in the lower half of the income distribution even more, and the relative net subsidy to labor supplied by high-wage workers would be lowered. This stimulus to the employment of low-wage workers is the best economic argument for a substantial increase in the base.

Our recommendations for increasing the extent of experience rating are not likely to be followed in their entirety. It is much easier politically to lower the minimum tax rate to zero than to remove the limit on the maximum tax rate. We have shown that raising the tax base improves experience rating when the minimum tax rate is zero. Consequently, if experience-rating schemes are changed mainly by more states adopting a minimum rate of zero on one or more schedules, increasing the tax base through federal legislation would have the desirable side effect of improving still further the degree of experience rating.

Both of these arguments lead to the conclusion that an increase in the UI tax base over a number of years until it equals the base for OASDHI ($15,300 in 1976) is desirable. Thereafter the base should be raised automatically each year so that the ratio of taxable payrolls to total payrolls does not begin the same erosion that was observed after 1972, when the $4,200 base became effective. The base should rise by the same percentage as the weekly wage. If that were done, the financial soundness of the system would be aided, since base-period earnings in many states depend upon weekly earnings. However, because increases in the OASDHI base are tied to wage increases in employment covered by that program, the reporting burden imposed on employers would be lightened considerably if the two bases were tied to the same indicator. Thus the best choice is to tie the UI tax base to the base for the OASDHI tax after providing by statute for its increase over a number of years until it is equal to the OASDHI base.

5

Other Economic Issues

The preceding chapters have focused on the effects of UI on unemployment and the distribution of income and their implications for policy changes. While these are clearly fundamental aspects of the system and should be major considerations underlying any changes, there are other areas in which the structure of UI impinges upon economic performance. These include the following: (1) the effect of interstate differences in benefits and taxes on flows of labor and capital between states, a topic central to the consideration of federal standards for benefit amounts; (2) coverage of workers. If some workers are not covered, as is now true, the effects of UI on the economy will differ because the uncovered sector provides an outlet for labor or capital that may be displaced from the covered sector; (3) eligibility for benefits. Of particular interest are the minimum employment duration and the question whether or not workers who quit voluntarily should receive benefits; and (4) adequacy of benefits. How high should benefit levels be, assuming we ignore their effects on incentives to seek work?

Interstate Differences in Taxes and Benefits

As noted in chapter 1, there are large differences among states in benefit levels and in the taxes used to finance them.

Not surprisingly, given that regular benefits are financed by taxes on employers in a particular state, taxes are highest where benefits are highest. With these simple facts in mind, we can examine how interstate competition affects the location of labor and capital. We will distinguish between the current system's impact and the possible effects of changes in benefits and/or tax rates on the location of jobs and industry.

A state that has high benefits over a long period is attractive to labor. Individuals born there, especially those who fear that their lack of skill will condemn them to frequent spells of unemployment, are more likely to remain than to migrate to otherwise similar states offering lower benefits. Likewise, potential migrants, particularly the young, who comprise a disproportionate share of all migrants, will move to those states in which UI benefits are most attractive. Indeed, this net migration (above what would have occurred in the absence of the UI program) is one of the factors leading to the relative decline in wages that prompted our conclusion that workers bear part of the cost of UI. Migration and interstate labor mobility cause wages to be lower than otherwise in states with high benefits. However, wages plus benefits are higher than in the program's absence, especially in states with high benefits. These phenomena arise so long as workers do not bear the entire burden of the tax.

Capital, which provides employment opportunities, is also mobile, although the fixed nature of investment in plant and equipment produces a very slow response to increases in the tax rate. Eventually, however, firms do respond, and as a result of UI the pattern of industrial location is shifted toward states with low benefits and taxes. Employers, as part of their adjustment to the imposition of UI taxes and their efforts to remain competitive, will locate where taxes are low.

The UI system as a whole affects the location of firms and workers. More capital than otherwise is located in areas where the tax (and benefit) rate is relatively low. More workers—especially less-skilled workers, who are more likely to experience unemployment, and workers who have a strong aversion to the uncertainties associated with the chance of unemployment—

are located in areas where benefits (and taxes) are high. Production in these areas uses more labor than in the absence of UI. All of these effects have been generated by UI since the 1930s. The extent of their impact is unclear, even though the directions are unambiguous.

The likely magnitude of the locational effects is best considered in the context of changes in the tax rate or in the benefit amount. Consider, for example, what might happen over a three- to five-year period if a state raised its benefits without raising taxes. Some additional migrants would flow in, and some potential emigrants would not leave, but the size of these two effects is likely to be small. Information about changed labor-market opportunities is disseminated slowly, so it takes some time before any reaction to the changed benefit levels occurs. Studies of interregional migration in the United States find that substantial relative changes in earnings produce only small changes in the direction and size of migration flows.[1]

An upper limit to the likely flow of migrants responding to higher state UI benefits is given by studies of migration in response to differences in welfare (AFDC) levels. Those who would potentially migrate in response to differences in welfare payments are likely to have little attachment to their home areas. Potential migrants responding to differences in UI benefits are still less likely to migrate, since the work required for eligibility for UI usually implies some attachment to a particular area. If the estimated effect of AFDC is small, we can be fairly certain that the effect of UI benefits is even smaller.

Available studies of the relationship of interstate migration to differences in welfare benefits suggest that in fact migration patterns are affected little by differences in welfare benefits.[2] Given the lack of information about job opportunities in other labor markets, as reflected in the small response of migration to income differences noted above, it is not surprising that the response to differential AFDC levels is small. Both findings suggest that the change in the working-age population in response to an increase in UI benefit levels is likely to be small. This is especially true over the three- to five-year time horizon that is probably relevant for policy.

If the tax rate on all employers in one state is raised (perhaps to replenish reserves depleted by a recession) and nothing else is changed, firms will locate in states that now appear more attractive (because labor costs there have dropped relatively). The response is very slow because most of the adjustment occurs through a deflection of some new investment away from the state. It is extremely unlikely that a business with a substantial investment in a plant that is not fully depreciated will close down merely because of an increase in the UI tax that raises labor costs by less than one percent (and thus raises total costs by a smaller percentage). Even potential new investments are not likely to be deflected to a great extent because the locational advantages of being near an isolated scarce item (coal sources or technically skilled labor) usually outweigh the small additions to labor cost. Unfortunately, there are very few studies of the response of investment flows to interstate differences in labor costs, and those available offer conflicting evidence on their effects on investment flows among regions.

This discussion suggests that increased UI taxes in a state do produce some advantages for employers because the benefits they finance induce workers to accept a somewhat lower wage. The rise in labor costs is less than the full increase in the UI tax. Furthermore, a state which is among the first to raise taxes will not suffer a serious loss of investment (and thus jobs) due to employers closing their plants or shifting their investment plans elsewhere. Rather, the probable result over a three- to five-year planning period is that almost all employment opportunities will remain in the state that has raised taxes. The cost of the UI tax increase will be borne partly by the state's labor force, partly by consumers of the state's products, and in the first year or two after the increase, partly by profits of firms located in the state. This last effect is probably the cause of business objections to increased tax rates.

Extent of Coverage

The extent of coverage of firms by the federal tax (assessed as .5 percent of the base in 1975) has generally determined the states' legal provisions for coverage. A worker is covered by the state UI system if his employer pays taxes on his wages, which he does as long as the worker is a paid employee whose work is subject to the employer's control or who works in an enterprise that forms part of the employer's regular business. In the matter of coverage there are two issues: (1) the cutoff size of covered employers and (2) the exclusion of employers belonging to an uncovered industry. While the program initially excluded those whose work force consisted of fewer than eight, today most state programs cover an employer if he has had one paid worker for at least twenty weeks in the calendar year.

Because of the gradual decrease in the cutoff size, due partly to the decreased administrative cost of keeping records on small employers, firm size is no longer an important issue, but uncovered industries remain a problem. Over its life the UI program has been broadened to include industries that previously were not covered. Table 7 presents the best available estimates of the extent of coverage of UI by industry for three years since the program's inception. The table shows, for example, that certain agricultural employees and some state and local government employees have become covered. The 1970 amendments extended coverage to a large number of service and state and local government employees, so that in 1973 covered employment and insured unemployment under regular state programs were 66 million out of a total of 86.1 million civilian workers employed or on layoff. The remaining 20.1 million people include 2.8 million federal employees and 600,000 railroad employees, both of which groups have separate programs. Furthermore, in 1973, 8.2 million people were self-employed or unpaid family workers. These considerations suggest that in 1973 only about 74.5 million workers were potentially coverable. Current provisions of the state UI laws are sufficiently broad to include approximately 88 percent (66/74.5) of the potentially coverable group. There is a possible expansion of only 12 percentage points, or 14 percent (12/88), in the extent of coverage. The only major areas for further extensions are agriculture, services, and state and local governments. (The coverage of employment [in numbers] closely approximates the coverage of wages: In 1973, 86 percent of all wages and salaries were in covered employment.)

Table 7. Percentage of Paid Employment Covered by State UI Programs, 1939, 1960, 1973, by Industry

Industry	1939	1960	1973
Agriculture	–	8.1	25.7
Mining	95.2	96.8	100[a]
Contract construction	83.5	91.9	100[a]
Manufacturing	94.7	99.2	100[a]
Transport, communications, and utilities	54.9	79.2	88.3
Wholesale and retail trade	83.2	92.4	100[a]
Finance, insurance, and real estate	71.8	87.7	98.8
Services	49.0	54.5	88.8
State and local government	–	5.8	25.2

SOURCES: Bureau of Labor Statistics, *Employment and Wages*, 1952, 1960, 1973; *Handbook of Labor Statistics*, 1975.

[a]Measured payroll employment is below covered employment because of differences in definitions of average employment and possible errors in the benchmarks used to estimate payroll employment in 1973.

If large segments of major industries are excluded from the program, as they were in 1975, all of the effects of UI on the economy discussed in the preceding three chapters will be modified somewhat. The larger the uncovered sector of the economy and the greater the potential mobility from the uncovered into the covered sector, the greater will be the share of the UI tax that firms can shift backward onto workers. Since some workers in uncovered employment will respond to higher benefits in covered employment by seeking jobs there, wages in covered employment will be lowered more than if this flow of labor were not possible. Thus, the total of wages and expected UI benefits would be below what it would be if coverage were complete.

Extension of coverage to additional industries prevents "leaks" of labor into the system that would otherwise increase the share of the taxes borne by covered employees. Additional coverage thus has important effects on income distribution even among those workers and industries previously covered. In particular, it makes the burden of the tax less regressive, for labor's share of the burden, which is currently likely to be regressive, is decreased.

An extension of coverage would also increase the extent of all the effects on unemployment discussed in chapters 3 and 4. Each effect was calculated under the assumption that the behavior of only three fourths of the civilian labor force (as measured in the monthly household survey) was affected. With broader coverage the effect would increase proportionately, although our discussion in this section suggests that the largest possible increase (resulting from universal coverage) would not exceed 14 percent. If coverage were universal, each unemployment effect calculated for the current system would rise by roughly this percentage.

The economic effects of changed coverage of UI are fairly clear. Limiting coverage to certain industries and to firms of certain sizes increases the extent to which workers bear the taxes used to finance benefits and provides hidden subsidies to those employers whose payrolls are not taxed. However, it is a difficult issue politically because extension of coverage would remove the advantages now enjoyed by excluded employers. It would raise costs of those currently exempt employers relative to those employers now participating in the system. Eventually this would increase their prices and lower their sales relative to those of employers who are already covered. The potential effect on unemployment is probably fairly small, though.

Eligibility—Requirements and Denial of Benefits

All states impose minimum requirements on earnings and/or weeks worked during the base period, designed to screen out those out-of-work individuals whose attachment to the labor force is not very strong. This issue is especially relevant to seasonal workers receiving UI. Since UI is intended to aid those unemployed who are seeking work, their eligibility should hinge upon their availability for work when their main (seasonal) employer does not need their services. Eligibility has two major aspects: First, what set of earnings-employment requirements should be placed on UI claimants to ensure the inclusion of as many as possible of those attached to the labor force while they receive benefits and the exclusion of as many as possible of those not so attached? This problem is posed by any endeavor requiring a rule that divides a population on a yes-no basis. Second, once these basic eligibility criteria have been determined, what restrictions should be placed on UI beneficiaries so that the incentive to continue drawing benefits (discussed in chapter 3) is mitigated? Here the issues are concerned with availability for work and the definition of suitable work. In both cases a substantial amount of legislation and case law exists, but there are some aspects on which economic analysis can shed new light.

Basically three earnings-employment criteria have been adopted by different states. The weeks-worked criterion (in New York and Oregon, among our examples) requires the claimant to have worked in each of a number of weeks in the base period, usually between fourteen and twenty. This requirement is designed to render ineligible some seasonal workers and others whose labor-force attachment is slight most of the year. The high-quarter-earnings criterion (in South Carolina, for example) states that the claimant must have earnings scattered throughout the rest of the year equal to between 25 and 50 percent (depending on the state) of what he made in his best quarter. There usually is also some requirement for a minimum earnings in the high quarter. While this criterion ensures that the worker was employed in at least two quarters, the earnings cutoffs are usually very low. In January 1975 the most stringent of the states using the multiple of high-quarter earnings (North Carolina) required at least $565 in earnings in the base period, work in two quarters, and total earnings equal to one and a half times high-quarter earnings. With a forty-hour work week and the minimum wage of $2.10 per hour, these minimum requirements could be met in seven weeks if the two-quarter requirement were met. The third criterion used (in Colorado and Massachusetts, for example) is minimum base-period earnings equal either to some multiple of the minimum weekly benefit amount, usually between thirty and forty, or to a minimum dollar amount of earnings. Often there is a requirement for earnings in two quarters. Here, too, it is possible for a worker earning the minimum wage to qualify quickly for the minimum weekly benefit. In the strictest state using the criterion of a multiple of weekly-benefit amount (Connecticut) this can be done in seven and a half weeks, again if the earnings are in different quarters.

In comparing these systems of determining eligibility we must examine which performs best by the criterion of excluding those out-of-work individuals who should be excluded (those not attached to the labor force) and including those who should be included (those attached). The term *labor force* is not precise, for it depends upon the work-seeking requirements placed on people who are not employed that serve to separate the unemployed from those out of the labor force. The best simple indicator is past employment. Representative data are not readily available on the work experience of the covered work force and insured unemployed, but there are data on the entire labor force and all unemployed people, as measured by the monthly household survey (Current Population Survey). Nearly 70 percent of nonagricultural workers in 1972 worked more than twenty-six weeks at full-time jobs. Similarly, another 19 percent held part-time jobs, most of them for a large fraction of the year. A very large majority of nonagricultural workers is thus strongly attached to the labor force. When we examine the composition of the experienced unemployed, those who worked in 1972, the picture is different. Among workers who were unemployed in March 1973 but held full-time jobs in 1972, only 59.7 percent had worked more than twenty-six weeks. If we also include those who worked part-time in 1972, of the unemployed who worked in 1972 only 60.3 percent of the males and 46.1 percent of the females worked more than twenty-six weeks. [3]

These data suggest that a large fraction of the experienced unemployed during the near-boom month of March 1973 were not very strongly attached to the labor force. Presumably, this fraction would be less when the ranks of the unemployed are swelled by job losers, as during a deep recession. Although these data include all workers, not just those covered by UI, and although some of those covered who worked a few weeks in 1972 were denied benefits for other reasons, there is good reason to conclude that during a cyclical boom a substantial fraction of the insured unemployed worked less than twenty-seven weeks in the base period.

This conclusion can be interpreted in two ways. If society wishes to have the UI system support some people, particularly seasonal workers, whose attachment to the labor force is marginal at most times, then the status quo is satisfactory. If, however, we view the main function of the UI system as providing support for those out-of-work members of society who are strongly attached to the labor force over the entire year, then an eligibility criterion that screens out more workers should be used.

In addition to the restrictions imposed by the earnings-employment criteria, conditions based on the cause of the worker's separation from his job also limit eligibility. The differences across states in denials of benefits for voluntary quits are immense, ranging in the five sample states in 1974 from 45 per 1,000 new claimants in New York to 262 per 1,000 new claimants in Colorado. Differences in the number of denials for misconduct are also quite large, and such denials are high where denials for quitting are high. The differences are caused to a large extent by variations in the state laws, but some further variations may be due to the harshness with which the laws are applied and the resources devoted by the state agencies to their enforcement.

Denial *rates* per thousand quits decrease in most states during a recession. For example, in fiscal year 1975 the rate for New York fell to 30 per 1,000 new claimants, and that for Colorado fell to 241 per 1,000. (However, the *number* of denials for quits rose in the 1973–75 recession. There were 217,000 denials nationwide in the second quarter of 1973, and 321,000 in the same quarter of 1975.) There are two possible causes of this decrease: (1) Fewer new claimants leave their jobs voluntarily during a recession, and (2) resources at the claims offices become strained and are increasingly devoted to paying benefits rather than to checking on the cause of the worker's separation. In a recession quit rates decline much more sharply than denial rates: The denial rate for quits nationwide was 28 percent lower in the second quarter of 1975 (a cyclical trough) than in the second quarter of 1973 (near a cyclical peak); the quit rate in manufacturing was 52 percent lower in the later period. This suggests that the major cause of the cyclical decline in denial rates is the shift in the composition of new UI claimants to include proportionately more job losers, not the possibly lax enforcement of eligibility requirements. UI claims officers do not seem to relax their vigilance in preventing this type of abuse at times when the claims load increases.

A crucial issue for workers denied benefits for quits or misconduct is the length of their disqualification from receiving benefits (the length of their waiting period). There is no "correct" length equally applicable to all workers who quit, and ad hoc determinations are clearly unfeasible and also likely to be inequitable. However, labor-market considerations should play a part in determining the appropriate length. Given the lack of job opportunities during a recession, a worker unhappy enough to quit very likely has a good cause for doing so. Also, a worker who quits without good cause in a recession will have difficulty finding a job. If he is still seeking work after a few weeks, it is a good indication of his attachment to the labor force. On the other hand, someone who quits without cause in a tight labor market when jobs are available and who is still not at work after a few weeks is more likely to be loosely attached to the labor force. These points imply that the waiting period should be shorter where and when the unemployment rate is higher.

The second major eligibility issue involves the degree to which administrative regulations in the UI system should provide beneficiaries an incentive to find and accept jobs. Availability for work and willingness to accept suitable work must be defined in any system that wishes to maintain incentives for its recipients to find work. There are some interesting economic issues in defining suitable work. These can be elucidated by considering the changes between fiscal years 1974 and 1975 in denial rates for refusal or unavailability for work. The denial rate for this cause declined as the economy moved into the recession, exactly as did the denial rate for quits. For example, the rate fell from 12 to 9 denials per 1,000 claimant contacts in New York and from 8 to 4 per 1,000 in Colorado. Unlike the case of denials for quits, however, there is no external information that indicates why the rate declined. Was it because enforcement of the work test was less harsh than before? Was it because the decline in labor demand induced by the declining demand for goods and services produced fewer suitable job openings? More basically, what is suitable employment?

Lower wages induce firms to hire more workers, other things being equal. A broader definition of suitable employment will then guarantee higher employment and lower unemployment than would a more narrow definition. Workers who previously would have accepted only those jobs paying the wage to which they were accustomed or in which they would use the skills they had accumulated would be induced to lower the wage they sought and to accept alternative employment. There is no doubt that such a get-tough policy would lower program costs, as it has in AFDC cases in selected localities. However, the evidence in chapter 3 suggests that the decrease in unemployment likely to be produced by denying UI benefits accounts for only a small part of recession-induced unemployment. Is the removal of this amount of unemployment worth the political price of forcing regular workers to accept low wages or jobs in which they would not use their skills? Even more important, is it economically efficient to risk locking a skilled worker into a job that fails to use his skill solely because society was short-sighted and required that he take a job during a period of unemployment in his regular work?

There are no easy answers to any of the questions about suitable work. Perhaps the best conclusion is that individuals on each side of the argument should be aware of some character-istics of the problem that appear to be widely ignored. Those who favor a narrow definition of suitable work should realize that its narrowness to some extent produces higher unemploy-ment and a general rigidity in the labor market and that skills will deteriorate just as fast when the worker is out of work as when he is working at an "unsuitable" job. Those who wish to see a broadening of the definition and application of the concept of suitable work should recognize that workers who take other jobs during a spell of unemployment thus cannot in many cases search for work as efficiently and are not so likely to return to their previous (highly skilled) jobs. They should also be aware of both the political difficulties inherent in their position and the evidence that accepting their view would have a fairly small effect on the unemployment problem. A far better political approach would be to restructure benefits to provide incentives that would reduce some of the extra unemployment now induced by UI.

Adequacy of Benefits

Determining the benefits a typical recipient *should* receive is inherently a matter of value judgment, at least if we are concerned with income replacement alone and ignore any possible incentive effects. Two alternatives exist: We must determine either some set of needs that individuals must have satisfied in order to live at some minimum level of human dignity or some a priori replacement rate on the basis of some norm agreed upon socially.

The first possibility, norm 1, can be handled objectively or subjectively. An objective approach would be to try to determine those expenses which the unemployed worker must incur to maintain body and soul while unemployed. This approach was used by the U.S. Department of Labor in its benefit-adequacy research in the 1950s, a series of studies of the budgets of UI recipients in six states. Expenses were classified as deferrable or nondeferrable, the second category comprising housing, clothing, food, and medical care. The norm was the worker's expenditure on these items before his period of unemployment, and his UI benefits were compared with this norm. This approach has serious logical problems. First, can an outsider determine which expenses are truly nondeferrable, that is, which expenses an individual or family regards as not being marginal? For example, depending on the duration of unemployment, most clothing purchases are easily postponable until a worker is reemployed. Similarly, medical care, be it a surgical procedure or treatment of a minor infection, can in many cases also be delayed without disaster (indeed, occasionally to the worker's benefit!).

The second and more serious problem is that this objective approach places its proponents in the position of arguing for an ever-declining replacement rate. If nondeferrable expenses constituted 80 percent of net income in the 1950s, then adjusting per capita incomes for inflation over twenty years would indicate that in 1975 these expenses constituted only 50 percent. If only $1,000 of expenditure was nondeferrable in the 1950s, no objective standard can claim that nondeferrable expenditures are now greater except for adjustments for inflation. As time passes, continued income growth ensures that nondeferrable expenses as a percentage of total income will approach zero. Unless one claims that the number of nondeferrable items increases, one is arguing for benefits to be fixed except for adjustments for inflation. If one claims that nondeferrables are growing over time, one ipso facto abandons objective standards and replaces them with a reliance on the subjective tastes of the moment. In short, either one takes the untenable position that needs are fixed for all time or one is forced away from needs determination (norm 1) to some replacement rate which society has agreed is the recipient's right (norm 2).

The only tenable argument for a constant replacement rate is thus the subjective one that society has agreed to guarantee its citizens (at least those qualifying for UI benefits) that their incomes shall not fall by more than some fixed fraction. This argument is precisely the one upon which a progressive tax structure must ultimately rest, namely, that society through the electoral process has expressed its tastes for an income distribution with certain characteristics. Only an ethical judgment of this sort can circumvent the logical problems that can arise in trying to define the appropriate level of income replacement.

Specific Policy Issues

Although our evidence shows that the effect of UI on *interstate competition* for jobs is small, there is very likely some effect, and the issue has substantial importance politically. Most of the deterrent to employers that is produced by high taxes is vitiated by changes in the supply of labor generated by the high benefits that those taxes finance. Nonetheless, as long as labor does not eventually pay the entire increase in UI taxes, employers in high-benefit states are placed at a competitive disadvantage. The greater this disadvantage, and the greater the extent of interstate differences in benefits and taxes, the more pressure corporations will apply to hold down benefits and taxes so as to equalize labor costs, and the greater the chance that legislators will respond to threats of industrial relocation.

One solution is to federalize the tax structure and abolish experience rating. This approach would remove the problem, since employers throughout the nation would pay the same tax rate. However, such a move represents a complete restructuring of the UI system and removes the beneficial effects on variations in employment that can be produced by a comprehensive experience-rating scheme. Interstate job competition can be handled much more readily by imposing federal standards for benefits. While there may be other and more important reasons for such standards, they probably would have the additional virtue of increasing the equality of UI costs among states. Because each state system is self-financing, this would in turn produce greater equality in UI tax rates across states. The equalization surely would not be complete because of interstate differences in unemployment rates and the likelihood that some states would pay benefits above the federal standard. But equalization would be greater than what now exists and would serve to calm the (probably unfounded) fears of an exodus of industry from high-benefit, high-tax states.

As noted earlier in this chapter, the potential for *extension of coverage* of the regular state UI systems is quite small, roughly only 9 million workers. These individuals are concentrated chiefly in state and local government, with most of the remainder in agriculture and service industries. Our discussion indicated that the exclusion of some industries from coverage under the UI program increases the regressivity of the UI tax by allowing flows of labor between the covered and uncovered sectors of the economy. Aside from other benefits that may accrue, extension could make the effect of the program in the rest of the economy more progressive. Furthermore, it would aid regular employees (in agriculture, for example) who are ineligible because the seasonal nature of much of the employment in their industry has induced Congress to refrain from extending coverage to them.

Although coverage should apply to all industries, there is one serious problem that has gone unrecognized: Most of the workers to be covered under any major extension will be state and local government employees. Unemployment rates among government workers, three fourths of whom are in state or local governments, were lower than in all other major industries in the years 1961–74 (except for mining in 1974). So long as state UI systems have minimum tax rates above zero, inclusion of state and local government under UI will produce a net addition to the pool of UI reserves in a state. Benefits paid over a period of years will very likely be so low that they will be exceeded by taxes. This means that the general taxpayer will be financing unemployment benefits in the rest of the state UI system, for UI taxes paid by governmental units come from taxes paid by citizens. This sort of cross-subsidy is undesirable in any event, but it is especially undesirable when a public agency that imposes taxes without any market test is involved. The problem would be obviated if experience rating were improved to allow wider variations in tax rates. That would enable UI taxes paid by state and local governments to approximate benefits more closely and thus would remove the cross-subsidies that would arise under the current experience-rating structures of most states.

Employment-earnings requirements for eligibility have been determined by each state for its own UI system, and this will probably continue. Without a complete federalization of UI any change in eligibility requirements must be on a state-by-state basis. Alterations will occur only if people's preferences for including or excluding workers whose labor-force attachment is slight undergo some changes. This is a political issue, but the methods for effecting the change once a political decision is made should be based upon economic analysis.

If eligibility is to be restricted, the eligibility criterion should be a minimum number of weeks worked during the base period and some minimum earnings in that period. Requiring at least twenty weeks of paid employment, each at or above some minimum weekly earnings or hours, as was done in five state systems in 1975, would serve to exclude many workers in seasonal industries whose attachment to the labor force is only seasonal. Using a multiple of high-quarter earnings or weekly benefits cannot exclude as many of these workers. (Haber and Murray show that in Oregon in 1960 a weeks-worked scheme produced 10 percent fewer workers qualifying for benefits, with the largest declines in agriculture and services, as compared with a method using a multiple of high-quarter earnings.)[4] The only argument against this scheme, assuming one wishes to exclude such individuals, is administrative. Employers file quarterly reports on covered earnings. Acquisition of information on weeks worked would require some modification of the reporting forms, but the rapidly decreasing costs of data processing suggest the administrative cost would be very small.

The unemployment costs of the program, the subsidy now provided to seasonal industries, and the desire to prevent UI from being viewed as a welfare program all lead to the conclusion that eligibility should be limited to those with at least twenty weeks of paid employment in the base period. The increase in seasonal unemployment noted in chapter 4 would be reduced, as would the subsidy now given to seasonal industries by the combination of imperfect experience rating and easy eligibility for benefits for seasonal workers. A worker who has only a seasonal attachment to the labor force could then be aided, if he qualified, by general assistance which is designed as a welfare program rather than by UI, which was not so intended. The purpose of the UI program would then be clearer, and its political acceptability would be even greater than it is now.

The appropriate degree of stringency in the definition of suitable work is in most cases a political issue. However, in the area of *interstate claims* for benefits some guidance can be provided. In the first quarter of 1975, for example, these claims accounted for 5 percent of total benefit payments under regular

95

state programs. Although interstate claims are useful for encouraging mobility from high- to low-unemployment areas, they also allow beneficiaries to "vacation" on UI benefits if the receiving state does not enforce work-seeking requirements. For example, in the winter quarter of 1975 Michigan and New York were liable for over twice as many interstate claims as they took, while Florida, the largest receiver of interstate claimants, was only liable for benefits to half as many interstate claimants as it handled. Since benefit costs are assessed against employers in the sending state, the receiving state has little incentive to apply a strict work test. The use of interstate claims as a way of enhancing labor mobility without allowing their abuse by vacationers should be encouraged. State officials should consider regulations allowing sending states to deny benefits to those interstate claimants who do not establish a residence in the receiving state. This would have only a small effect on total program costs, but the potential for abuse by interstate claimants and the resulting public criticism of the program are so high as to make these proposed regulations fairly important.

6

What Do We Know and What Should Be Done?

Our knowledge of the economic effects of unemployment insurance has been severely limited by two interacting factors. First, the legal and administrative provisions of the systems are so complex and the interstate differences so varied that many economists have been discouraged from working in the area in the past twenty-five years. Second, even when interest has been present, the data needed to provide answers have in most cases been lacking. For these reasons, until recently we have known very little about the economic effects of the system, and that lack of knowledge has guaranteed that economic considerations have had a minimal impact on the policy debate.

What We Now Know

Our findings have covered so many areas that it is worthwhile to summarize them here.

1. It is probable that employers ultimately pay at most only a small fraction of the taxes that finance UI benefits, for they are able to shift part of the tax burden backward onto labor and most of the rest forward onto their customers. Nonetheless, this process does not begin immediately, and for at least the first year after an employer's UI tax rate is increased he bears most of the increase.

2. UI payments are distributed nearly proportionately among families ranked by their other income, except that the poorest families receive few UI benefits, while the very well-to-do also receive a relatively small share.

3. The combined effect of taxes and benefits on the distribution of income is small. Benefits are distributed more equally than are incomes, but because of the limitation on the tax base, the part of the tax burden supported by workers is probably borne most heavily by low-wage labor.

4. The amount of income, net of taxes, transportation costs, and so forth (including fringe payments) replaced by UI benefits is below two thirds for individuals who just qualify for the maximum benefit; for most individuals it is probably close to 50 percent.

5. The system has numerous effects on the measured unemployment rate. These include changes in the duration of unemployment of UI recipients, in the number of people seeking work, and in the labor-force status of recipients during a recession.

6. Exhaustions of benefits vary cyclically and in systematic ways among states, with more exhaustions occurring in states that have a variable potential duration of benefits. These differences produce insured-unemployment rates that are higher in states with a longer average potential duration of benefits.

7. The limits on tax rates in most state experience-rating systems make additional layoffs less costly for as many as one third of employers. This leads to implicit subsidies from employers with stable work forces to those employers whose work forces are not stable. These cross-subsidies distort the pattern of production toward those items for which employment variations are greater.

8. The limits on experience rating give employers an incentive to increase the extent of seasonal variation in their work forces. This produces more spells of unemployment and thus a higher unemployment rate on the average over the year.

9. Regular state UI benefits have offset about 10 percent of the decline in purchasing power that has occurred in recessions since 1945.

10. The limit on the tax base (to $4,200 in most states in 1975) decreases the employment of low-wage workers relative to that of high-wage workers more than it would if the base were higher.

11. Interstate differences in benefits and taxes are substantial, but their effects on differences in labor costs partly offset each other. To the extent that they do not, they do produce some (probably very small) shift in the location of capital-using heavy industry away from states having high UI taxes and benefits. It is usually several years, however, before any tax increase produces an effect on the location of industry.

12. Limitations on the coverage of UI increase the share of the tax borne by labor and affect the program's operation in covered employment.

13. A substantial fraction of the experienced unemployed work very few weeks during the year prior to their current spell of unemployment. Determining eligibility for UI benefits based on high-quarter or annual earnings enables these workers, whose attachment to the labor force often is apparently quite weak, to qualify for benefits.

In addition to these specific points, we have calculated the magnitudes of each of a number of effects of the current system of regular UI benefits on the civilian unemployment rate. For some of these the direct evidence is fairly strong, while for others the best available evidence has been pieced together from diverse sources. To gauge the overall effect on unemployment, these separate effects can be combined. Our bases for comparison are a low unemployment rate of 4 percent and a recession unemployment rate of 7.3 percent, each assumed to occur in the absence of the regular unemployment-insurance programs. To make the comparisons, we combine the percentage increase in the number of spells of unemployment induced by the increased seasonal variation in employment; the percentage increase in duration of unemployment; the induced increase in the labor force at full employment; and the effect on macroeconomic activity during a recession induced by increased UI benefits.

Table 8 lists these effects as percentage-point increases in the unemployment rate. Our best estimates are that the civilian

99

unemployment rate is .7 percentage points higher at low unemployment and .45 percentage points higher during a deep recession than it would be in the program's absence. Expressed differently, if low unemployment in the late 1970s is 4.7 percent, it could be as low as 4 percent if regular UI benefits are not paid. The .7 figure implies that nearly one third of the insured unemployed during low-unemployment periods would be at work (.7 divided by 2.2, the hypothetical insured-unemployment rate based on the assumption that insured unemployment as a fraction of civilian unemployment would be .47, as in 1969). This estimate may appear high, but most of the induced unemployment is based on the well-documented effect of UI benefits on the duration of unemployment when labor markets are tight.

Table 8. Estimated Total Effects of Regular State UI Programs on the Civilian Unemployment Rate (in percentage points)

Change	At low unemployment	At high unemployment
Real	+.61	+.27
Measured	+.10	+.51
Macroeconomic effect	—	−.33
Total	+.71	+.45

These estimated total effects mask several important considerations. First, if we believe that individuals would save sufficiently to provide for their periods of unemployment or that the macroeconomic effects of UI benefits operate through monetary channels alone, there is no net effect of UI on the magnitude of cyclical fluctuations in unemployment. If so, induced unemployment in a recession is .78 percentage points, not the .45 estimate listed in table 8.

A second consideration, however, is that the estimates of the amount of induced unemployment include some measured unemployment, reflecting shifts into unemployment by people who otherwise would have been out of the labor force. These shifts do not represent wasted human resources. If we are concerned only with real effects of the program, we can conclude that it induces only .61 and .27 percentage points of unemployment at low and high unemployment, respectively (assuming for the moment that the true macroeconomic effect is zero).

Third, the induced real increase in unemployment may be overstated because of behavioral and institutional effects. In the absence of publicly provided UI benefits, some private scheme of unemployment insurance would probably arise. (The existence of privately financed Supplementary Unemployment Benefits above regular UI benefits suggests that people wish to reduce the variability of their incomes and that removing UI benefits would produce a sharp growth in private benefit plans.) Any such plan, no matter how it is financed or how the benefits are structured, would provide greater incentive for unemployment than would occur in its absence. The institutional factor is that workers forced off UI would find their incomes partly maintained by other transfer programs. These often contain schedules that reduce payments as earnings increase, and thus they too contain disincentives to work that increase unemployment. Abolishing UI would lower unemployment only to the extent that potential private substitutes and current welfare programs are more successful in avoiding disincentives. Public programs can perhaps be altered or cut, but any cut in UI would certainly spur the growth of private substitutes.

These effects represent only what would occur if the U.S. economy did not contain a regular UI program structured as ours was in 1975. They do not allow us to make any statements about the true severity of recessions in the 1970s as compared with the recessions of 1948, 1954, 1958, or 1961, except to the slight extent that permanent extensions of coverage in 1970 broadened the impact of the program. They merely imply that part of the unemployment we observe is induced by the current structure of unemployment insurance. They do suggest, however, that further extensions of the program—of coverage, benefit amounts, or potential duration of benefits—will produce increases in the unemployment rate. Thus the permanent program of triggered Extended Benefits and the temporary programs enacted in 1974 and 1975 produce some (probably small) addition to the amount of unemployment induced by UI.

Our best estimate is that the temporary programs added between .3 and .4 percentage points to the unemployment rate of 1975.

The induced unemployment should be construed partly as an investment made by society to subsidize job search, which can result in a more efficient labor market. In part, however, it is a needless diversion of human resources away from their best uses, produced by the combined effects of legislated accretions to the program and changes in the labor market and the tax system. Whether the real and measured effects are too large or too small depends on one's beliefs about the importance of efficiency in the labor market. Observers who believe that any inefficiency in the labor market must be removed, regardless of its other beneficial effects, will regard these effects as too large to justify the program; those who feel that society should be willing to pay a high price to aid the unemployed or that UI offsets the effects of other inefficiency in the economy will consider these effects small. The appropriate question for this second group is, can the same improvement in the stabilization of incomes of the experienced unemployed be achieved without the likely loss in efficiency?

Suggestions for Change

Without altering the fundamental structure of the program, much of the inefficiency and inequity it now produces can be removed. Our suggested changes do not tamper with the essential diversity of the program that Becker has called "competitive socialism." [1] They do not alter its reliance on experience-rated taxes and its attempt to replace the income losses of out-of-work individuals who are attached to the labor force. Instead, they streamline the program and steer it to meet the goals that it was designed to meet, and they abandon secondary aims that have to some extent interfered with its primary endeavors and caused much resentment.

Our program for UI reform, summarized below, entails changes in a number of areas. Each program change affects the budget for UI. Because UI is just one of several income-maintenance programs, if adopted each would eventually have an impact on these others as well.

Data and Information

This and other studies cannot answer many important questions about UI because the data are not available. At the very least, the following data should be made available on a regular basis for a selected sample of states:

1. Tax rates, tax bills and benefit costs by industry, and variations in tax rates within each industry would enable more precise inferences to be made about who eventually pays the UI tax.

2. More information about individual beneficiaries similar to the data that have formed the basis for some of the studies of the effects of benefits on the duration of unemployment listed in table 4 is needed on a continuous basis. Such data would allow one to deduce beneficiaries' labor-force status over several years prior to their receipt of UI benefits and thus to gauge the extent of their attachment to the labor force.

3. Published monthly data on a current basis on exhaustions, claimants, amounts of benefits, and average duration for each particular UI program are needed. Much of this information is now unpublished or otherwise inaccessible.

Financing

1. The tax base should gradually be increased until it equals the base for Social Security ($15,300 in 1976). This would remove some of the tax burden that now falls on low-skilled employees and would somewhat ease their chances of finding employment.

2. Through amendments to Federal UI legislation that would deny them the revenues for administration raised by the federal tax, states should be induced to expand tax-schedule limits, ideally until the minimum rate is zero and there is no maximum

rate. This expansion would lessen or even remove the cross-subsidy that now occurs and would reduce unemployment by raising the costs of layoffs to many firms. A perfect experience-rating scheme can be used to finance all charged benefits in a state.

3. Noncharged benefits should be financed by a flat-rate tax on covered employees. A rate based on previous years' experience in the state can be set that will keep the fund solvent over periods of five years, on the average. When deficits occur either on noncharged benefits paid out of taxes on employees or on charged benefits (when they increase rapidly during a recession), they can be funded through the same system of advances now used.

Coverage

Coverage should encompass all sectors of the economy. If most employment in a sector is highly seasonal, the seasonal employees can be excluded by tightened eligibility requirements. Year-round employees should not be denied coverage because many of their coworkers are seasonal employees.

Benefits—Miscellaneous Recommendations

1. Eligibility should be based on weeks of work during the base period, and some minimum-earnings requirement should also be applied. At least twenty weeks of work, each at a minimum weekly earnings, should be required. This would eliminate mainly those recipients whose demonstrated attachment to the labor force is usually quite weak.

2. The ceiling on maximum benefits should be removed, partly because individuals whose earnings are above average should not be denied the same percentage replacement of income lost as lower-wage individuals, partly because this is only fair if the tax base is raised substantially.

3. Dependents' allowances should be discontinued. They make the extent of benefits under UI, a work-related program, conditional on family size, which is not related to work. Furthermore, in the few states where they are offered, they can

raise the net replacement rate so sharply that the incentive to seek work may be weakened.

4. Benefits for partial unemployment can provide an incentive for the fully unemployed to seek some work. The incentive exists, however, only when the loss of benefits is less than the extra earnings received. Partial-benefit schedules must be revised to guarantee that this incentive is maintained over the entire range of the schedule.

5. Potential duration should vary with the claimant's base-period earnings up to the maximum potential duration.

Benefits—Amount

Because UI benefits are not taxed, replacement rates, based on lost earnings only, seem to exceed the 50-percent gross replacement rate facing most beneficiaries. Our findings imply, however, that when all factors are counted, net replacement rates for the average beneficiary are generally around 50 percent, which is not greatly different from gross replacement rates. If our recommendation is adopted and eligibility is based on weeks worked, most of the beneficiaries who are least closely attached to the labor force will be screened out. The incentive to seek work will thus be very strong, as will the degree of attachment to the labor force among the remaining low-wage beneficiaries. Only among one group (the high-wage unemployed eligible for increased benefits if the benefit ceiling is removed) will net replacement rates approach 100 percent, for only for them is the tax rate on earnings fairly high.

These considerations suggest, first, that gross benefits should be raised to two thirds of weekly earnings during the base period for all beneficiaries; second, that UI benefits should be taxed exactly as are earnings; and third, to effect these changes, benefit standards should be legislated at the federal level, and the tax code should be changed to permit the taxation of transfer income.

These recommendations and those on eligibility, maximum benefits, and dependents' allowances made above would (1) increase net replacement rates for the low-wage unemployed who have a demonstrated attachment to the labor force; (2)

leave the average beneficiary essentially unaffected; (3) reduce net replacement slightly for workers barely at the current benefit maximum; and (4) increase net replacement slightly for those few unemployed workers whose current benefits replace much less than 50 percent of their wage loss because their base-period earnings are so high. These alterations are similar to recent changes made in Canada except that they include provisions for tightened eligibility requirements, whereas Canada eased these. They would probably lower the program's effect on unemployment by screening out those persons most likely to enter the labor force because of the inducements of future UI benefits and those others for whom the effect on duration of unemployment is probably greatest.

Benefits—Maximum Potential Duration

During the recession year 1975 approximately $4.6 billion in extended UI benefits (Extended and Federal Supplemental Benefits) was disbursed. These payments were authorized partly by the 1970 UI amendments and partly by the emergency legislation of 1974 and 1975. If we wish to extend benefits for up to sixty-five weeks in a recession, the extension should be triggered automatically to avoid possible legislative inertia. But the basic question is, Should such benefits be paid out at all? Would the $4.6 billion not have been more useful in some other income-maintenance or job-creation scheme?

Consider two alternatives: paying $4.6 billion a year in extended benefits or spending the same amount on a public-service employment program (either federal or shared). The employment program would have an advantage to the extent that (1) society values the output produced by its enrollees; (2) it does not displace spending by lower units of government; (3) enrollees maintain their skills better than they would if they were not working and were drawing extended UI benefits; (4) enrollees, especially the unskilled, develop both specific and general job skills as a result of the program; and (5) enrollment in the program does not hinder a participant's job search as labor demand rises at the end of the recession.

The value society places on the output of an emergency public jobs program is not known. Was the WPA "leaf-raking," or was it a major investment in the infrastructure of the U.S. economy? While the question cannot be given a conclusive answer, it should remind us to look carefully at the projects proposed under any emergency jobs program. If only a small part of spending by lower governments is displaced, the stimulatory effect of the allowances paid to enrollees will not be lost. While some displacement is likely, it can be minimized if the program is operated on a federal basis rather than through shared revenue.

Comparing the alternatives of enrolling in a jobs program or continuing to draw UI benefits beyond twenty-six weeks, it is fairly easy to conclude that during a recession there is little successful job searching in any case. If so, there is little fear that putting an individual into a public jobs program instead of paying him extended benefits will greatly reduce his chances of finding private-sector employment or increase the rate at which his skills deteriorate.

Taking these considerations together, we recommend that all extended-benefit programs be phased out and that a federally-run work-project program be created. Enrollment in this program should be limited to individuals who have exhausted their regular UI entitlement. Allowances should equal the weekly benefits the enrollee would have received had he still been drawing unemployment compensation. (The hourly wage should be the minimum wage, and weekly hours should then equal the ratio of the person's weekly UI benefits to the minimum wage.) This ensures that an incentive to seek private-sector employment is maintained for most enrollees. Participants should be allowed to remain enrolled so long as they wish, provided they perform the tasks required of them. Funding, on a federal basis, should cover the allowances of all exhaustees of regular UI benefits who wish to enroll in the public employment program.

These recommendations are made in full awareness that they represent a sharp departure from the recent trend toward an ever-greater maximum potential duration of UI benefits. (Late in 1975 Senator Jacob Javits proposed extending benefits through seventy-eight weeks of unemployment.)[2] Nonetheless, this trend is dangerous, for the UI system assumes more and more welfare-program aspects. The evidence suggests that if a person has not found work in a recession after twenty-six weeks of unemployment, he is not likely to do so thereafter unless demand conditions improve. Offering him the opportunity for dignified work in the public sector enables him to support himself, maintains the incentive to seek reemployment, and gives the rest of society some output in return for the resources transferred from taxpayers to UI recipients. At low unemployment the program would be very small. Few people exhaust benefits, and it is likely that many of those who do would prefer to seek higher paying, private-sector employment or drop out of the labor force.

Conclusions

A major conclusion of most studies of government programs is that more research is needed. If that recommendation is valid for other employment and welfare programs, it is even more valid for UI. The importance of the economic issues for fashioning appropriate policies and the current lack of a satisfactory resolution of most of them make the need for increased, more careful research crucial.

The UI program has operated for nearly forty years as a "first line of defense" against income losses produced by individual and mass unemployment. With the implementation of the changes we have suggested it can continue to do so. However, it cannot function simultaneously as a second, third, and fourth line of defense without limiting its ability to succeed in its primary mission. It should not be used as a vehicle for maintaining the incomes of individuals whose labor-force attachment is slight, nor should it be the vehicle by which the incomes of the long-term unemployed are maintained. It is now successful in meeting its basic goal, and with the modifications suggested here its success can be maintained and its small, negative effects on economic performance removed.

Notes

Chapter 1

1. Bureau of National Affairs, *Daily Labor Report,* 5 September 1974, pp. AA-1–AA-6.
2. For example, the segment on CBS, *Sixty Minutes*, vol. 8, no. 19, 25 April 1976. See also Martin Feldstein, "Unemployment Compensation."
3. For a thorough description and history of UI in this country consult William Haber and Merrill G. Murray, *Unemployment Insurance in the American Economy.*

Chapter 2

1. Calculated from Joseph M. Becker, *Experience Rating in Unemployment Insurance*, p. 343.
2. John H. Pencavel, "Some Labor Market Implications of the Payroll Tax for Unemployment and Old Age Insurance."
3. Raymond Avrutis, *How to Collect Unemployment Benefits.*
4. Virginia Employment Commission, Poster B-29A.
5. Richard A. Lester, *The Economics of Unemployment Compensation.*
6. Edward M. Gramlich, "The Distributional Effects of Higher Unemployment."
7. Stephen Wandner, "Unemployment Insurance and the Duration of Unemployment in Periods of Low and High Unemployment."
8. William Papier, "Standards for Improving Maximum Unemployment Insurance Benefits."
9. U.S. Chamber of Commerce, *Employee Benefits, 1973* (Washington, D.C.: U.S. Chamber of Commerce, 1973).
10. Gregory Mills, "Evidence of the Counter-cyclical Response of Income Transfer Programs."
11. Mathematica, Inc., *A Longitudinal Study of Unemployment Insurance Exhaustees.*
12. Martin Feldstein, "Unemployment Compensation."
13. Joseph A. Pechman and Benjamin A. Okner, *Who Bears the Tax Burden?*

109

14. Papier, "Standards for Improving Maximum Unemployment Insurance Benefits."
15. 94th Congress, H.R. 8614, and H.R. 8366.

Chapter 3

1. *New York Times*, 20 September 1975, p. 39.
2. Donald I. Mackay and Graham L. Reid, "Redundancy, Unemployment and Manpower Policy."
3. Robert L. Crosslin, "Unemployment Insurance and Job Search."
4. Arnold Katz, "Acceptance Wages of the Longer-Term Unemployed."
5. Paul Burgess and Jerry Kingston, "Unemployment Insurance, the Job Search Process and Reemployment Success."
6. Arlene Holen, "Effects of Unemployment Insurance Entitlement on Duration and Job Search Outcome."
7. Ronald G. Ehrenberg and Ronald L. Oaxaca, "Unemployment Insurance, Duration of Unemployment and Subsequent Wage Gain"; Ronald M. Schmidt, "The Determinants of Search Behavior and the Value of Additional Unemployment."
8. Kathleen Classen, "The Effects of Unemployment Insurance."
9. Bureau of National Affairs, *Daily Labor Report*, 13 August 1975, pp. E-1–E-4.
10. Joseph E. Hight, "Insured Unemployment Rates, Extended Benefits and Unemployment Insurance Exhaustions."
11. James S. Hanna; Robert T. Butler; and John P. Steinman, "The Socioeconomic Impact of Extended Benefits."
12. See Merrill G. Murray, *The Duration of Unemployment Benefits*, for a summary.
13. Mathematica, Inc., *A Longitudinal Study of Unemployment Insurance Exhaustees*.
14. Bureau of National Affairs, *Daily Labor Report*, 21 February 1975, pp. A-12–A-13.
15. See, for example, *New York Times*, 26 September 1976, p. 36.
16. U.S. Council of Economic Advisors, *Economic Report of the President, 1975*.
17. 94th Congress, H.R. 8366.
18. Murray, *Duration of Unemployment Benefits*; Mathematica, *Longitudinal Study*.
19. Glen G. Cain and Harold Watts, *Income Maintenance and Labor Supply*.
20. U.S. Council of Economic Advisors, *Economic Report*.
21. Raymond Munts, "Partial Benefit Schedules in Unemployment Insurance."

Chapter 4

1. Peter Eilbott, "The Effectiveness of Automatic Stabilizers"; Wilfred Lewis, *Federal Fiscal Policy in Postwar Recessions*; George Rejda, "Unemployment Insurance as an Automatic Stabilizer"; George von Furstenberg, "Stabilization Characteristics of Unemployment Insurance."
2. M. O. Clement, "The Quantitative Impact of Automatic Stabilizers"; Rejda, "Unemployment Insurance."
3. Eilbott, "Effectiveness of Automatic Stabilizers."

4. Clement, "Quantitative Impact."
5. Ibid.
6. Joseph M. Becker, *Experience Rating in Unemployment Insurance*, pp. 336–37.
7. Ibid.
8. Charles Warden, "Unemployment Compensation."
9. James O'Connor, "Seasonal Unemployment and Unemployment Insurance."
10. Becker, *Experience Rating*, pp. 88–89.
11. Ibid., p. 113.
12. Warden, "Unemployment Compensation."
13. Becker, *Experience Rating*.
14. See memorandum of 10 January 1975 from Under Secretary of Labor Richard F. Schubert to Assistant Secretary William Kolberg.
15. *Wall Street Journal*, 12 December 1975, p. 14.

Chapter 5

1. Samuel Bowles, "Migration as Investment"; and the references therein.
2. For example, David Kaun, "Negro Migration and Unemployment."
3. Calculated from Bureau of Labor Statistics, *Work Experience of the Population in March 1972*, Special Labor Force Report, no. 162.
4. William Haber and Merrill G. Murray, *Unemployment Insurance in the American Economy*, p. 255.

Chapter 6

1. Joseph M. Becker, *Experience Rating in Unemployment Insurance*.
2. Bureau of National Affairs, *Daily Labor Report*, 19 December 1975, p. A-14.

111

Bibliography

Avrutis, Raymond. *How to Collect Unemployment Benefits.* New York: Schocken Books, 1975.

Becker, Joseph M. *Experience Rating in Unemployment Insurance.* Baltimore: Johns Hopkins University Press, 1972.

Bowles, Samuel. "Migration as Investment." *Review of Economics and Statistics* 52 (November 1970): 356–62.

Burgess, Paul, and Kingston, Jerry. "Unemployment Insurance, the Job Search Process and Reemployment Success." Mimeographed. Unemployment Insurance Service, U.S. Department of Labor, 1974.

Cain, Glen G., and Watts, Harold. *Income Maintenance and Labor Supply.* Chicago: Rand McNally, 1973.

Chapin, Gene. "Unemployment Insurance, Job Search and the Demand for Leisure." *Western Economic Journal* 9 (March 1971): 102–7.

Classen, Kathleen. "The Effects of Unemployment Insurance: Evidence from Pennsylvania." Mimeographed. ASPER, U.S. Department of Labor, 1975.

Clement, M. O. "The Quantitative Impact of Automatic Stabilizers." *Review of Economics and Statistics* 42 (February 1960): 56–61.

Crosslin, Robert L. "Unemployment Insurance and Job Search." Mimeographed. Department of Economics, Mississippi State University, 1975.

Duesenberry, James; Eckstein, Otto; and Fromm, Gary. "A Simulation of the U.S. Economy in Recession." *Econometrica* 28 (October 1960): 749–809.

Ehrenberg, Ronald G., and Oaxaca, Ronald L. "Unemployment Insurance, Duration of Unemployment and Subsequent Wage Gain." *American Economic Review* 66 (December 1976).

Eilbott, Peter. "The Effectiveness of Automatic Stabilizers." *American Economic Review* 56 (June 1966): 450–65.

Felder, Henry. "Job Search: An Empirical Analysis of the Search Behavior of Low-Income Workers." Mimeographed. Stanford Research Institute, 1975.

Feldstein, Martin. "Unemployment Compensation: Adverse Incentives and Distributional Anomalies." *National Tax Journal* 27 (June 1974): 231–44.

Gramlich, Edward M. "The Distributional Effects of Higher Unemployment." *Brookings Papers on Economic Activity* 5 (1974): 293–336.

Haber, William, and Murray, Merrill G. *Unemployment Insurance in the American Economy.* Homewood, Ill.: Richard D. Irwin, 1966.

Hanna, James S.; Butler, Robert T.; and Steinman, John P. "The Socioeconomic Impact of Extended Benefits." Mimeographed. Nevada Employment Security Department, 1975.

Hight, Joseph E. "Insured Unemployment Rates, Extended Benefits and Unemployment Insurance Exhaustions." *Proceedings of the Industrial Relations Research Association* 28 (December 1975): 242–49.

Holen, Arlene. "Effects of Unemployment Insurance Entitlement on Duration and Job Search Outcome." Mimeographed. Center for Naval Analyses, Arlington, Va., 1976.

Katz, Arnold. "Acceptance Wages of the Longer-Term Unemployed." Mimeographed. Center for Naval Analyses, Arlington, Va., 1974.

Kaun, David. "Negro Migration and Unemployment." *Journal of Human Resources* 5 (Spring 1970): 191–207.

Lester, Richard A. *The Economics of Unemployment Compensation.* Princeton: Princeton University Industrial Relations Section, 1962.

Lewis, Wilfrid. *Federal Fiscal Policy in Postwar Recessions.* Washington, D.C.: Brookings Institution, 1962.

Lininger, Charles A. *Unemployment Benefits and Duration.* Ann Arbor: University of Michigan Institute for Social Research, 1963.

Mackay, Donald I., and Reid, Graham L. "Redundancy, Unemployment and Manpower Policy." *Economic Journal* 82 (December 1972): 1256–72.

Marston, Stephen T. "The Impact of Unemployment Insurance on Aggregate Unemployment." *Brookings Papers on Economic Activity* 6 (1975): 13–49.

Mathematica, Inc. *A Longitudinal Study of Unemployment Insurance Exhaustees.* Princeton: Mathematica, 1976.

Mills, Gregory. "Evidence of the Counter-cyclical Response of Income Transfer Programs." Mimeographed. Office of Income Security Policy, U.S. Department of Health, Education and Welfare, 1975.

Munts, Raymond. "Partial Benefit Schedules in Unemployment Insurance: Their Effect on Work Incentive." *Journal of Human Resources* 5 (Spring 1970): 160–76.

Murray, Merrill G. *The Duration of Unemployment Benefits.* Kalamazoo, Mich.: W. E. Upjohn Institute, 1974.

O'Connor, James. "Seasonal Unemployment and Unemployment Insurance." *American Economic Review* 52 (June 1962): 460–71.

Papier, William. "Standards for Improving Maximum Unemployment Insurance Benefits." *Industrial and Labor Relations Review* 27 (April 1974): 376–90.

Pechman, Joseph A., and Okner, Benjamin A. *Who Bears the Tax Burden?* Washington, D.C.: Brookings Institution, 1974.

Pencavel, John H. "Some Labor Market Implications of the Payroll Tax for Unemployment and Old Age Insurance." Mimeographed. Department of Economics, Stanford University, 1974.

Rejda, George. "Unemployment Insurance as an Automatic Stabilizer." *Journal of Risk and Insurance* 33 (June 1966): 195–208.

Schmidt, Ronald M. "The Determinants of Search Behavior and the Value of Additional Unemployment." Mimeographed. School of Management, University of Rochester, 1974.

U.S. Council of Economic Advisors. *Economic Report of the President, 1975.* Washington, D.C.: U.S. Government Printing Office, 1975.

113

von Furstenberg, George. "Stabilization Characteristics of Unemployment Insurance." *Industrial and Labor Relations Review* 29 (April 1976): 363–76.

Wandner, Stephen. "Unemployment Insurance and the Duration of Unemployment in Periods of Low and High Unemployment." Mimeographed. Unemployment Insurance Service, U.S. Department of Labor, 1975.

Warden, Charles. "Unemployment Compensation: The Massachusetts Experience." In *Studies in the Economics of Income Maintenance*, Otto Eckstein, ed., pp. 73–93. Washington, D.C.: Brookings Institution, 1967.

Library of Congress Cataloging in Publication Data

Hamermesh, Daniel S.
    Jobless pay and the economy.

    (Policy studies in employment and welfare;
no. 29)
    Bibliography: p. 112.
    1.   Insurance, Unemployment—United States.
I.   Title.
HD7096.U5H275   368.4'4'00973   76–47369
ISBN 0–8018–1927–X
ISBN 0–8018–1928–8 pbk.